Praise

"A must read not only ~~[barcode]~~ trauma or other neurological diseases but also for their families and health care providers."
—Susan Glacken, MA, LPCC

"An excellent and clearly written book which will be useful for patients, their families, and members of the medical community who treat them."
—J. Mitchell Simson MD, MPH, FASAM

How My Brain Works

How My Brain Works
A Guide to Understanding It Better and Keeping It Healthy

Dr. Barbara Koltuska-Haskin

Golden Word Books
Santa Fe, NM

Library of Congress Control Number 2020932825

G
W
B

How My Brain Works. Copyright © 2020
by Dr. Barbara Koltuska-Haskin
All rights reserved
Printed in the United States of America

No part of this book may be used or reproduced in any manner whatsoever without written permission except in the case of brief quotations embedded in critical articles and reviews. Send inquiries to Golden Word Books, 33 Alondra Road, Santa Fe, New Mexico 87508.

Published by Golden Word Books, Santa Fe, New Mexico.
www.GoldenWordBooks.com

ISBN 978-1-948749-61-9

To Norbert Christopher

Contents

Foreword xi
Preface xiii
Acknowledgments xv

Part I: Evaluating the Brain

1. Neuropsychology: A Little Bit of History 3
2. What Is Neuropsychology, and What Is Neuropsychological Evaluation? 5
3. What Is the Purpose of Neuropsychological Evaluation? 8
4. What Neuropsychological Evaluation Consists Of .. 9
5. The Power of Clinical Observation 12
6. How Neuropsychological Evaluation Can Help You, the Reader of This Book 14
7. How Neuropsychological Evaluation Can Help Your Family 16
8. How Neuropsychological Evaluation Can Help If You Are a College Student 23
9. How Neuropsychological Evaluation Can Help If You Have Difficulty Completing Your Duties at Work 26
10. How Neuropsychological Evaluation Can Help Your Primary Care Physician, Neurologist, Psychiatrist, and Other Medical Care Providers 28
11. How Neuropsychological Evaluation Can Help Your Therapist 37
12. How Neuropsychological Evaluation Can Help Case Managers and Case Coordinators 40

13. The Exit Session: Discussing the Results of the Evaluation and Recommendations 42
14. Mastering Your Strengths 52
15. How to Deal With a Loved One Who Has "Brain Problems" 54
16. Menopause and Memory 57
17. How to Find a Neuropsychologist 60

Part II: Brain Health

18. The Power of Proper Nutrition 63
19. The Importance of a Good Night's Sleep 86
20. The Power of Physical Exercise 88
21. The Importance of Practicing Yoga 91
22. The Power of Active Learning and Positive Brain Stimulation 92
23. Gardening: Food for Body, Mind, and Spirit (and Very Good Brain Exercise) 100
24. Living in the Present: The Power of Mindfulness ...104
25. Practice Gratitude for Mental Uplifting 106
26. The Practice of Meditation 109
27. Getting in Touch with Your Spiritual Self 116
28. The Power of Kindness and Compassion 118
29. The Power of Inspiration 120
30. Strive for Progress, Not Perfection 124
31. Concluding Remarks 126

References 128

As long as you are breathing, there is more right with you than wrong with you.
—Jon Kabat-Zinn

Foreword

I WAS EXPOSED TO THE VALUE OF NEUROPSYCHOLOGICAL testing early in my medical career. I have ordered it frequently over the last forty years when I needed more information concerning complex psychological and psychiatric disorders. As Dr. Koltuska-Haskin points out, this type of testing can be extremely helpful when working with complex patients who have a variety of coexisting medical and psychological disorders such as PTSD, chronic pain disorders, depression and anxiety, traumatic brain injuries, and substance use disorders.

As an addiction specialist, I have found neuropsychological testing to be a critical tool in developing an effective treatment plan, especially for patients with substance use disorders who are not responding well to their therapies.

Dr. Barbara Koltuska-Haskin's book is actually two books in one. The first part is an excellent in-depth discussion of what neuropsychology is and what a comprehensive neuropsychological evaluation can accomplish. It's written primarily for patients and their families. However, because it is so practical and lucid, I plan on using it as a reference source for our medical students and residents so that they too will understand the benefit of such testing.

The second part of the book focuses on brain health and includes practical, personal, and positive advice about how to preserve and enhance brain function. Included are the known benefits of proper sleep, exercise, nutrition, and meditative practices such as yoga. The reference list is quite extensive and will allow others to delve deeper into academic and research topics should they wish.

All in all, this is an excellent and clearly written book which will be useful for patients, their families, and members of the medical community who treat them.

—J. Mitchell Simson MD, MPH, FASAM,
Associate Professor, University of New Mexico School of Medicine

Preface

HAVE YOU EVER WONDERED IF YOUR MEMORY IS THE SAME as several years ago or found yourself making "stupid mistakes"? Do you sometimes search for the right word or feel like your thinking is slower than in the past? You talk to your friends or your spouse about it, but either they haven't noticed anything or they brush it off, blaming it on simply "getting older." You still have a feeling that you're not as sharp as a few years ago, so you go to your doctor. The doctor schedules an MRI or CT scan, but it comes back normal. After a while, you may start thinking there's something wrong with you that only you can see, and wonder if you're "going crazy."

Relax! You're not going crazy, and this book is just for you.

If you have any doubts about your everyday functioning, such as memory lapses, difficulty processing information, problems with concentration, or difficulty finishing tasks, dwelling on your difficulties may cause anxiety, sadness, or depression. Instead, schedule an appointment with a neuropsychologist and complete a neuropsychological evaluation. What you think is your problem may not be accurate. For example, you may think that your memory is failing, but memory complaints aren't necessarily memory problems. Once your evaluation is completed, you may find out that you have other difficulties, such as attention/concentration problems or difficulties in planning and organizing, but your memory may be within the normal range for your age.

You don't need to wait until you have memory problems or have had a head injury or a stroke to see a neuropsychologist. You may want to know how your brain is working at present to program your career or improve cognitive functions that are important in your private or professional life.

The purpose of this book, which comes from my more than thirty years of experience as a neuropsychologist, is to explain how neuropsychological evaluation can help you understand how your brain is working, in order for you to reach your full potential and/or to help you heal if you're recovering from brain trauma or other brain-related problems or diseases. I'll share with you some of my favorite ideas and mind practices for improving and maintaining your brain health, ones that I use in my clinical practice and also in my everyday life. Most of my patients say that these ideas and practices have been helpful. I hope they can help you as well.

I always talk to my patients about a healthy lifestyle. This includes healthy eating, exercising, mindfulness, gratitude, and getting enough sleep. Your brain doesn't work in isolation. The healthier your body, the better your brain will function.

I truly believe that *food is our medicine*. Therefore, I'll share with you some of my favorite healthy meals recipes. My lifelong hobby has been organic gardening and organic cooking, using produce mainly from my garden. I'll also share with you how to use commonly grown weeds, herbs, and edible flowers to enhance the flavor of your meals so you won't need to use heavy sauces full of chemicals, calories, and artificial flavor enhancements. As a bonus, you may lose some weight in the process.

I hope this book will inspire you to take the first step on the road to a healthy, fulfilling, and successful life.

—Dr. Barbara Koltuska-Haskin

Acknowledgments

WRITING A BOOK IS A LONG AND LABORIOUS PROCESS which cannot be accomplished without help and support from family, friends, colleagues, and literary and publishing professionals. There are many people who helped me accomplish my project. I am very grateful to all of them.

First and foremost, I want to thank my patients, who have been my toughest teachers and inspiration for over thirty years of my professional career. On the personal side, I want to thank my husband, Ed, for his love and support. I also want to thank my friends and professional colleagues who have read my manuscript and given me valuable advice, especially Dr. Betsy Williams and Susan Glacken, LPCC. I also want to thank Dr. Mitchell Simson for writing a very thoughtful Foreword.

Many thanks to William Greenleaf from Greenleaf Literary Services for his excellent editorial work and helpful advice. I also want to thank Liz Trupin-Pulli from JET Literary Associates for her very helpful advice. Special thanks goes to my publisher, Marty Gerber from Terra Nova Books and his team for patiently working with me during the publishing process.

I also want to thank three people whom I have never met but who inspired me and gave me the impetus to start working on this book. First, I want to thank the late Dr. Wayne Dyer for his everlasting wisdom. Many thanks also to Oprah Winfrey for her brilliant and thought-provoking Super Soul Sunday series which "opened many doors in my mind" and helped me see many aspects of humanity from totally different perspectives.

This book probably would never have been completed if not for author Elizabeth Gilbert. I was "writing" it in my mind for about three years before I decided to sit down and actually start. I have a very busy practice, and caring for my patients has always been my priority. I felt that I never had enough time to start working on the book and had been pushing it out of my tasks-to-do list. However, several years ago, I saw Gilbert on TV talking about aspiring writers complaining on Facebook that they have busy lives and no time to start writing. "Hmm, that's me," my inner voice said. Gilbert had brilliant advice for all those people, something like: "If you are really in love, no matter how busy you are, you will always find time to see your lover. So fall in love with your book and find the time to write it. Assign time every week. It can be as little as fifteen minutes." That did it for me. The same day, I decided that every Monday evening, I would work on my book and try to write about one page. I kept this promise to myself, trying not to miss a Monday evening. It took over three years, but I did it. Thank you, Ms. Gilbert!

Part I
Evaluating the Brain

~1~
Neuropsychology: A Little Bit of History

THE TERM "CLINICAL NEUROPSYCHOLOGY" WAS FIRST USED by Sir William Osler in 1913 (Lezak 1995) and appeared in the work of Karl Lashley in 1936. The science of neuropsychology evolved from neurology and psychology, and became an independent discipline in the 1940s.

The major work in the field of neuropsychology was done by Alexander R. Luria (1902–1977), a brilliant Russian physician and neuroscientist. His ideas about how the brain works originated from his clinical practice during World War II working with Russian soldiers who had suffered traumatic brain injury (TBI). Many of these injuries had been caused by gunshot wounds, and thus tended to be confined to one area of the brain.

Luria observed the wounded soldiers as they recovered. He knew where in the brain the injury was, and what his patients could not do as a result. He kept detailed notes and put the information together to formulate groundbreaking theories about brain functioning, which he first presented in his 1962 book, *Higher Cortical Functions in Man*. This has been recognized as the principal book establishing neuropsychology as a medical discipline of its own (Homskaya 2001). Luria later supplemented it with his most important and well-known book, published in 1973: *The Working Brain*.

Luria describes three constantly coactive functional systems in the brain. The first is the arousal system, which resides in the brain stem structures and regulates cortical tone and alertness. The second system is responsible for receiving, processing, and storing information and resides in the posterior cerebral cortex (at the back of the head). The third system, which programs, regulates, controls, and evaluates the complex form of human psyche and behavior, resides in the anterior cerebral cortex, the part of the brain called "frontal lobes." He also divided the second and third systems into primary, secondary, and tertiary functional areas.

On the basis of Luria's research, theory, and clinical practice, the Luria-Nebraska Neuropsychological Battery was developed by Charles J. Golden, Arnold D. Purisch, and Thomas A. Hammeke. First published in 1980, it is still commonly used by neuropsychologists as a screening and evaluation tool.

We also need to mention the work of Lauretta Bender and Brenda Milner (since there were not that many women in the field many years ago). Bender (1897–1987) was an American child neuropsychiatrist who developed the Bender-Gestalt Test which is still commonly used to assess visual perception and visual-motor skills. Milner (born in 1918) is a brilliant British-Canadian neuropsychologist who has done a lot of innovative and important research. At ninety-nine, she was still walking every day to her her scientific work at McGill University in Montreal!

I also have to mention the work of David Wechsler (1896–1981), an American psychologist of Romanian origin who created the Wechsler Intelligence Scale and Wechsler Memory Scale which are now in their fourth edition and commonly used in clinical practice. Worth mentioning is the work of Edith Kaplan and Harold Goodglass in the area of aphasia (speech-language problems after brain trauma). They developed the Boston Diagnostic Aphasia Examination battery a long time ago, and it is still commonly used. There were many other important scientists in the field of neuropsychology, e.g., Mishkin, Pribram, Teuber, Zangwill, and others. It would be too long a list to mention all of them. Their work can be "Googled" if someone is interested.

Modern neuropsychology evolved into several disciplines such as clinical, experimental, forensic, and pediatric. Probably, the most developing discipline right now is experimental neuropsychology.

~2~
What Is Neuropsychology and What Is Neuropsychological Evaluation?

WHAT IS NEUROPSYCHOLOGY? WHAT IS NEUROPSYCHOlogical evaluation? Most people have no idea, and many health care professionals wouldn't be able to answer these questions correctly either.

Let me explain it simply. Neuropsychology can be seen as a bridge between medicine and psychology. In fact, to become a neuropsychologist, one has to have a good background in both clinical psychology and medical sciences such as neuroanatomy, neurophysiology, and neurology. Also, knowledge about common illnesses that affect brain functioning, such as anemia or thyroid disease, is helpful. The more medical knowledge a neuropsychologist has, the better he or she can serve patients, because most of them, especially the elderly, come with complicated medical problems affecting the functioning of their brains.

If you want to go on the journey to improving your brain functioning, you need a "road map" of that functioning, and neuropsychological evaluation is that map. It tells which of your cognitive functions are average for your age and which are better or much better. It will also tell which are below average for your age or which are compromised and by how much (mild, moderate, severe). Most important, you can use the knowledge about your brain to improve your everyday functioning, reach your life goals, and improve or overcome cognitive problems such as memory, attention, or verbal problems. It will also help you understand how emotional problems such as depression, anxiety, or mood swings affect your cognition and what you can do to help yourself in these areas.

Neuropsychological evaluation is performed by a neuropsychologist who holds a doctoral degree, usually a Ph.D. or Psy.D.

If the neuropsychological evaluation can be seen as a road map to the understanding of someone's brain functioning, then the neuropsychologist can be seen as a guide on that road. The practitioner uses specialized testing to examine your brain function, as well as careful clinical observation (a powerful tool that we'll talk about later), and also reviews your medical records.

Based on the results of the comprehensive evaluation, the neuropsychologist will recommend how to work on improving and maintaining your brain functions. The evaluation should be a positive and uplifting experience. When you finish it, you should have a good idea of how your brain works and how you can compensate for, maintain, or improve your cognitive functioning. Most important, you should feel empowered to start the journey of improving your overall brain functioning. I always tell my patients, who are usually referred to me by their physicians or therapists, that I'm doing the neuropsychological evaluation *mainly* for them so they can understand how their brain is working and start the journey toward a better future with better brain functioning.

Knowing how your brain works is powerful, because what you *don't know* could hurt you. If you know what works well in your brain and what does not—for example, which of your brain functions are strong and which are weaker—you can learn to use the good parts to compensate for those that aren't so good. For example, a person's good visual memory can be used to facilitate compromised verbal memory. You can also do specific mental exercises to work on improving the part of your brain that isn't functioning well. (I'll talk about this later.) You may also find out that high anxiety affects your attention and concentration abilities. Therefore, treating this anxiety can improve your attention and concentration.

The results of the evaluation will guide physicians or therapists to prepare the most suitable treatment plan for you, one tailored to your needs throughout the whole therapeutic process, which can take from weeks to years, depending on the severity of your case.

The neuropsychological evaluation is unique, and only a neuropsychologist can perform it. Brain imaging techniques such as MRIs and CT scans sometimes show an anatomical problem in the brain but do *not* explain how this affects a particular patient. Each brain is somewhat different structurally, and an abnormal MRI doesn't always mean that the patient has significant problems. Conversely, the patient often has a lot of cognitive problems but a MRI or CT scan that is normal.

Neuropsychological evaluation is considered a medical benefit by most insurance plans and is usually covered. It's also covered by Medicare, Medicaid, and most Medicare Advantage plans. The evaluation, which is crucial to understanding a person's brain functions, is significantly underutilized by health care professionals. However, once used, the referring professionals greatly appreciate its value for diagnostic and treatment purposes.

I need to mention here an area of caution: In our current era of advanced technology, you can find some neuropsychological assessments online. Even the best of these, though, are only screening devices and should not be used to diagnose yourself. Please don't take them if you suffer from anxiety or depression. Lower scores may result not from cognitive problems but emotional ones. Doing poorly on online tests may worsen your emotional state, unnecessarily magnify your fears, and cause increased sadness and anxiety. It's essential that your evaluation be done by a qualified neuropsychologist who can choose appropriate instruments for your specific concerns, interpret the findings, and offer recommendations and support.

~3~
What Is the Purpose of Neuropsychological Evaluation?

THE MAIN PURPOSE OF A NEUROPSYCHOLOGICAL EVALUAtion is to assess your cognitive functioning, or how your brain is working. Important questions that need to be answered include:

- How is your memory?
- Do you have attention/concentration deficits?
- How well do you process verbal and nonverbal information?
- Can you effectively problem solve?
- Do you have sound judgment?

Also, your emotional functioning, such as depression, mood problems, and anxiety, need to be assessed because any problems in these areas affect the way your brain processes information. Most of the time, the magnitude of your emotional problems and of your cognitive problems are related. For example, the more severe your depression is, the more difficulty you'll have with processing information, memory, or attention/concentration.

The neuropsychological evaluation is usually performed to assess the cognitive consequence of brain traumas, brain disease, or severe mental illness. For the past several years, with a growing number of people affected by early dementia, some people want to know if they're showing any signs of cognitive problems or decline and what they can do to prevent such problems from getting worse.

~4~
What Neuropsychological Evaluation Consists Of

To clear up confusion and reduce anxiety in patients, I'll begin by explaining what the neuropsychological evaluation does *not* consist of: any brain imaging such as MRIs, CT scans, or electroencephalographs (EEGs), which are used to rule out seizure activity in the brain; or any invasive procedures such as brain biopsies. The tests used during the neuropsychological evaluation include paper and pencil, visual (such as color blocks or matrices), and auditory or hands-on measures of various domains of cognitive functioning related to the referral questions. The neuropsychologist can also use tests that have been created for computer use.

The comprehensive neuropsychological evaluation consists of:

- A clinical interview, which also includes review of available records;
- Testing of cognitive functioning;
- Testing of personality and emotional functioning;
- Scoring and interpreting the results;
- An exit session, which includes discussing test results and giving detailed recommendations; and
- Preparation of a comprehensive report.

As you can see, the evaluation requires time and effort on both sides—the examinee (patient) and the examiner (neuropsychologist)—and may take from two to four appointments. It can also be done in one long appointment with a lunch break, but that may be quite tiring for some patients, and I avoid doing it. I want to get true results of the patient's functioning without fatigue being a factor.

Also, a neuropsychologist who sees you just once may not get a complete picture of your functioning. For example, it may be a "bad" day when you're tired or "under the weather," and you'll be performing below your normal level. Or you may be coming out of your vacation and have an unusually "good" day. This is even more important in people with mood disorders. They may be extremely depressed one day and "kind of normal" or even hypomanic the next. It's important for the examiner to observe these changes, since they will help him understand overall functioning and have a better knowledge of how mood may be affecting cognitive functioning.

To give you some idea of what to expect, here is what the parts of the comprehensive neuropsychological evaluation are like:

- **The clinical interview.** This is the first step, an important part of the evaluation. It is the only time the examiner will ask detailed questions about your symptoms and history, including your developmental history. This interview is the source of the clinical questions the examiner will be investigating during the testing part of the evaluation. For example, if you have memory problems, it's important to know what kind. You'll be asked to describe them as well as you can, when they started, and whether they're getting worse. If you've suffered brain trauma or have other neurological problems, you'll be asked about your functioning before the causative event and symptoms and duration afterward.

Part of the clinical intake is to review records from other health care providers or hospital stays, if available. These are a good source of information about your medical, psychiatric, psychological, and social history,

- **Testing of cognitive functioning.** This usually includes your verbal and nonverbal abilities, memory, attention/concentration, executive functioning, and motor functions. Which of the many tests a neuropsychologist chooses to administer depends on the presenting problem. For example, if you have memory problems, tests such as Wechsler Memory Scale-Fourth Edition, Memory-for-Designs Test, etc. will be the most important part of the evaluation. However, the comprehensive evaluation will cover many aspects of your cognitive functioning to find out if there are any other problem areas such as attention/concentration, executive functioning, processing speed, etc.

The examiner can also use neuropsychological batteries such as Luria-Nebraska or Halstead-Reitan or create his or her own battery from many available tests to better assess your cognition. If you have questions about the tests administered during your evaluation, you shouldn't hesitate to ask.

- **Testing of personality and emotional functioning.** This is an important part of the evaluation, since your emotional functioning may significantly affect your cognitive functioning. Depression, anxiety, and mood problems that frequently develop after brain trauma or other neurological problems do not facilitate healing, and need to be carefully diagnosed and treated by your providers (physicians, therapists, and other health care professionals).

A neuropsychological evaluation should be a positive experience. It requires time and effort, but when you finish, you should have a feeling that it was worth it. You should have an understanding of how your brain is working and be empowered to make positive changes in your life. You should believe that you're finally on the right road to self-improvement and self-fulfillment. It's your responsibility to stay on that road as much as you can. If you find this difficult, you can get help through such things as lifestyle changes, therapy, or medications, which I'll discuss later in the book.

The neuropsychological evaluation should be performed in a friendly, accepting, and nonjudgmental atmosphere. You should feel that you can trust your examiner. If you don't feel that way, find another one.

~5~
The Power of Clinical Observation

THE MOST IMPORTANT PART OF NEUROPSYCHOLOGICAL evaluation is the careful observation that takes place from the first encounter with the patient, throughout the clinical interview and testing sessions, to the last or exit session when the tests results and recommendations are discussed. Clinical observation is a powerful tool that guides the examiner's diagnostic process. The skillful clinician takes cues from the patient's general appearance: neat clothing or untidy presentation; the way the patient greets the examiner (cheerful, anxious, or guarded), posture (normal, erect, or slumped), the way the patient is walking (unsteady gait, limping, slow), the way the patient is talking (normal, fast and loud, or slow and soft), and the way the patient answers questions.

The skillful examiner looks carefully at the skin, face, complexion, and hair. For example, a pale complexion may be a sign of anemia, which causes fatigue. Thinning hair may suggest underactive thyroid, which can cause cognitive problems, anxiety, or depression. Usually, patients who have serious and sometimes undiagnosed medical problems look tired and fragile. Any of the physical problems noticed by the examiner, which the person may not be fully aware of, could be a contributing factor to cognitive problems and need to be checked by a physician. A vibrant complexion and a lot of energy may mean that cognitive problems don't have a serious medical background.

Careful observation of the patient during the initial interview determines what kind of cognitive and emotional problems the patient may have and how they need to be tested. For example, if the patient is quite distractible, constantly changing his position in a chair and playing with the pencil and eraser, then the emphasis needs to be on testing attention/concentration abilities. If the patient is constantly searching for words and forgets questions or goes off topic, then the emphasis needs to be on testing memory.

Observation during testing is also important because the way the patient answers test questions and solves testing problems provides information about the nature of the problems experienced in everyday life. It can be a source of hypotheses regarding what kind of cognitive and emotional problems make the patient less successful than the patient would like to be. For example, the examiner is carefully observing if the patient diligently works on solving the testing problem or gets easily frustrated and gives up. Does the patient use the same strategy that already has failed or does he try to find a new one? Does the patient rush through the task, not paying attention to details? Does it take him much longer than normal to complete tasks?

Because of the importance of observation, I would recommend that you find an examiner who administers tests personally instead of using a technician, or important information coming from observation may be lost. Technicians are now commonly used, mainly in teaching hospitals and multispecialty clinics, because this lets the organization serve more patients and is more cost-effective. Unfortunately, using technicians may not be the best option for you, especially if your problems are complex.

~6~
How Neuropsychological Evaluation Can Help You, the Reader of This Book

KNOWING HOW YOUR BRAIN IS WORKING IS POWERFUL, BEcause you can make informed decisions about your everyday life and your future. Most people don't really know what their level of functioning is or what their special talents are, and aren't using them to the best of their ability. Some questions to ask: Is my I.Q. average or above average? Do I learn better by seeing or listening?

Below is a powerful example from my clinical practice of how the neuropsychological evaluation can help.

* * *

Michael was a thirty-four-year-old chronic alcoholic. Referred by family members, he was single, lived with his mother, and did summer work for minimum wage. He had a high school education but had dropped out of college because of his addiction. He had no meaningful relationships in his life and felt lonely and socially isolated. He looked somewhat disheveled and was quite anxious when he came to me. He didn't know what to expect.

To make him feel more comfortable, I explained what we would be doing. When testing was completed, he found out to his surprise that his intelligence was superior and his nonverbal abilities were very superior. His other cognitive functions were also quite good. However, he had chronic, severe, and untreated depression that he had medicated with alcohol for many years.

It turned out that depression ran in his family, but the other family members were getting treatment that he himself had refused. Finding out that his brain was still functioning quite well despite years of untreated depression and alcoholism was a life-changing experience for him. He said he wanted to begin treatment and start to make positive changes in his life.

We began with scheduling a family meeting, since family involvement is crucial in the treatment and recovery process. I emphasized that his especially good cognitive functioning should not be wasted and needed to be preserved. During the meeting, we discussed detailed recommendations and came up with a plan. I called it "the brain preservation program for Michael." This included referring him to a psychiatrist for a medication evaluation and to a therapist to treat his depression and addiction.

He agreed to attend A.A. meetings and return to college when medication had stabilized his depression. The last I heard, he was doing much better and had returned to college.

~7~
How Neuropsychological Evaluation Can Help Your Family

PEOPLE WHO HAVE EVEN MILD COGNITIVE PROBLEMS THAT are undiagnosed, such as attention deficit disorder (ADD), trouble processing information, or short-term memory problems, may not only have difficulties in their everyday life but frequently, their problems can make their family life quite challenging. Finding out what kind of cognitive issues they have and how to treat and deal with them in everyday life can be a life-changing experience, not only for that person but also for the family.

For example, people with attention deficit hyperactivity disorder (ADHD) who have attention/concentration problems can also be quite disorganized and forgetful. They're frequently accused of being lazy or of not investing in a relationship. Family members may often be upset with them because they have to constantly pick up after them, and are irritated by their apparent lack of responsibility. When the evaluation has been completed and test results are explained to the patient and family, it's frequently eye opening, especially for the family.

* * *

I vividly remember the case of a professional man who was brought to my office by his wife, who was at the end of her rope. She said that she was tired of constantly reminding him of everything, picking up after him, and fixing his mistakes such as not showing up for medical appointments or going to his primary care physician instead of his dentist. He, on the other hand, said he was fed up with her constant complaining. Testing showed quite severe ADHD. To my surprise, both husband and wife felt relieved. We discussed treatment options in detail, including long-term therapy and pharmacological intervention.

* * *

Another interesting case was a man who called our office asking for help and wanting to know what was wrong with him. Despite his successful career in science and technology, his marriage was falling apart, and his wife wanted a separation. She felt he didn't listen to her or understand her needs, and that she was unable to communicate with him.

When the testing was completed, it turned out that his nonverbal abilities were superior but verbal only average, and his emotional vocabulary was somewhat deficient. He had difficulty verbalizing his emotional states and also in recognizing the emotional states of others. When confronted, he had a tendency to intellectualize. He also seemed to sense more than he was able or willing to verbalize. His way of communicating was sufficient in his professional environment but not in a personal relationship.

Again, explaining how his brain worked greatly relieved both husband and wife. He wanted to stay in the marriage and was committed to doing anything to help it. With detailed testing results, they were referred to a couples therapist to help them effectively communicate in the relationship. The man called back some time later and said he had learned a lot about himself and was optimistic that he could save his marriage.

It's important to understand that for a child or adolescent with ADHD or ADD, the task of doing homework, especially if it involves several subjects, may be overwhelming. Frequently the child simply doesn't know where to start and how to progress to completion, and would rather do anything else. The pile of schoolbooks and papers seems like an iceberg or a mountain that cannot be conquered. Therefore, homework isn't done, despite the consequences. This often results in low grades, parental irritation, a power struggle, and family fights.

One solution is to help the child or adolescent prepare a written plan of how to go about completing homework or other difficult tasks. This can be done during therapy. The therapist can also prepare a flowchart that will guide the youngster from start to completion when doing homework. If parents do the supervising, they need to be nonjudgmental, offering no criticism for mistakes but praise for accomplishments. If parents have the financial resources, I recommend hiring a tutor for some time until the child learns how to do homework and other important tasks independently.

I frequently have to explain to parents that avoidance of homework and other school or home problems is a result not of the child's being lazy but of cognitive problems that need to be properly diagnosed and treated. ADHD or ADD is a complex diagnosis and should be done by a trained professional, preferably a child and adolescent neuropsychologist. Once your child is diagnosed, it's time for remediation. Therapy should always be the first step. The therapist will work on developing coping skills that the child can apply to real-life situations to effectively handle her or his problems.

The most important lesson for the child is to learn to have a cognitive approach to problems rather than an emotional one. What I mean is that if a problem appears, the first response should not be fear, sadness, crying, or self-esteem issues such as thinking, "I'm not smart enough or good enough to do that." Rather, the cognitive approach can be summarized by saying, "Where there's a problem, there's a solution. I just need to find the right one." This kind of approach to problem solving is empowering to the patient and will benefit him or her throughout life.

The therapist can also teach your child specific individualized techniques to deal with difficulties in everyday life, including schoolwork. ADHD medications can also help. They've been on the market for a long time, a lot of research has been done, and they are relatively safe. Some physicians may recommend fish oil and other supplements. A growing body of research indicates that meditation is a powerful tool. To teach a child to meditate may be a challenge but is very much worth the effort. Some research suggests that it may be as effective as medications but without the side effects, so it's worthwhile to start meditation with your offspring, since it will also benefit you, the parent. Goldie Hawn, the movie star, is successfully teaching meditation techniques in schools, even elementary. You can also be successful. It just requires commitment and patience.

*   *   *

I once saw a woman who told me her third-grade son had recently been diagnosed with ADHD after having struggled a great deal in school. She wanted to understand the condition better to be able to help him more effectively, and she wondered if she herself had some form of ADHD, although she didn't remember having any major problems in school.

What a brave mother, I thought.

The testing showed that she had a mild form of ADHD which did not require treatment, since it didn't appear to be significantly interfering with her life. However, she became sad thinking that she might have given her son the condition. We spent time talking about it, and I emphasized that instead of blaming herself, she needed to concentrate on finding him the most effective help. Fortunately, many clinic and private practitioners specialize in treating ADHD in school-age children. The mother needed to explore them and find which would be most suitable. I emphasized that after she found the most suitable treatment setting, she needed to make sure that her son liked it and was eager to attend treatment sessions. Otherwise, it wouldn't work and would be a waste of time and money. It may take time to find the right therapy, but it's worth the effort. I mentioned that if she had more problems related to guilt, she could benefit from therapy herself.

Traumatic brain injuries (TBIs) are a major problem that can affect family life. Frequently, the TBI happened in childhood or adolescence, and the patient has almost forgotten the accident or never connected it to current problems. Unfortunately, most patients who have suffered from TBI have never been evaluated by a neuropsychologist, and nobody has explained to them the connection between their brain trauma and their difficulties functioning in everyday life. Some people recover quite well from their early TBI and can have a successful and fulfilling professional and family life. For others, that's not the case.

* * *

One of my patients, Harry, was referred to me by his physician when he was in his forties. He had gotten married a year before for a second time, and mentioned more than once that he loved his wife and wanted to stay in the marriage. However, he and his wife were having trouble communicating and were frequently getting into fights. Harry said his wife accused him of being lazy because he had difficulty finishing household projects. She felt that he didn't listen to her and didn't respect her.

During the initial interview, he reported memory problems and attention/concentration problems. When asked about a history of TBI, he paused for a moment and said that, in fact, he had suffered a TBI in a motorcycle accident when he was nineteen. He believed that he had recovered quite well because he had no visible scars.

The neuropsychological evaluation revealed multiple problems in almost all areas of Harry's cognitive functioning. During the exit session, when the results were discussed in detail with him and his wife, it was explained how his cognitive problems affected his everyday functioning.

His wife burst into tears when she realized that he wasn't purposely disregarding or disrespecting her but in fact was having problems due to his TBI. Because Harry had not been referred for a neuropsychological evaluation after his TBI, he was never told how it had affected his functioning.

At their exit session, detailed recommendations were provided. It was emphasized that he required written, step-by-step instructions on how to go about home projects and shouldn't be given more than two-step verbal instructions at a time. Harry and his wife were referred for couples therapy to continue working on improving their communication skills and their relationship. I heard from him later, and he said that he and his wife were doing much better.

* * *

Another difficult family situation involved a spouse who had just suffered a TBI. In my practice, I frequently see a husband brought in by his wife. It may be because males are more frequently victims of motorcycle or car accidents. After their hospitalization, they're released to go home, and their wives have to deal with a variety of not only medical and cognitive problems but also emotional problems or sudden mood changes and anger outbursts. Frequently, the wife will report that she cannot recognize the man she married because he changed so much after the brain trauma.

Severity of the injury and the overall medical condition before the trauma are important. The person who was healthy before and had no alcohol or substance abuse problems is usually able to recover better and faster than someone who has multiple medical problems, addiction problems, or previous brain traumas.

* * *

Mark was brought to me for a neuropsychological evaluation by his wife after a referral from his family physician. He had suffered a brain injury three months earlier in a car accident. His wife reported that he'd changed so much after the accident that she couldn't recognize the man she had married several years ago. The couple had two preschool-age children, and she felt as if all of a sudden, she had a third child in the house who required a lot of care and attention. For example, he would get jealous when she paid attention to the children instead of him.

What was most concerning to her was that his behavior became quite unpredictable and sometimes unmanageable. Everything seemed to irritate him, even small things. When he started an argument, it was difficult to calm him down.

He had frequent mood swings and got into rages in front of the children, which frightened them. He also had a disregard for safety.

A recent incident had frightened her and made her determined to look for help. Mark had started an argument about a trifle while she was driving him to his physical therapy appointment, and she could not calm him down. He told her he was getting out of the car and tried to open the door while it was still moving. His wife had to stop the car and let him out. Fortunately, they weren't on a busy street. After a while, she calmed him down, and they drove on to his appointment.

During the clinical interview in our office, Mark frequently interrupted his wife and at some point became argumentative with her. When I was doing the mental status assessment, he had difficulty following directions and became somewhat belligerent. It became obvious that completing the testing would be extremely difficult. I urgently recommended that Mark be seen by a psychiatrist for medication evaluation to deal with his quite severe mood problems. I told him and his wife that we would continue testing when he was stable on medication.

They agreed, and he returned later, much more cooperative. The testing was completed and showed many cognitive and emotional problems. It was recommended that he continue to remain in the care of his psychiatrist and attend therapy on a weekly basis for an extended time. I also recommended that his wife seek therapy to help her better deal with the challenges that Mark's brain injury brought to her life and the family's life.

~8~
How Neuropsychological Evaluation Can Help If You Are a College Student

IF YOU FINISHED HIGH SCHOOL WITHOUT MAJOR PROBLEMS and now are having difficulty passing classes in college, instead of becoming anxious, depressed, discouraged, and dropping out, get yourself evaluated. And parents, if you find that your child is failing classes and you have to deal with a crying young person on the phone, the same advice applies. Keep in mind that finishing college and getting a degree is an investment in the future that will pay off throughout life, so you need to find out what the problems are and how they can be solved. If you are the young person in question, you may have some mild cognitive issues that weren't visible in high school but caught up with you in college when you had to do much more learning in less time. I'm not talking here, though, about a situation in which failing classes result from abusing alcohol or other drugs, since this requires a different type of evaluation and intervention.

If your neuropsychological evaluation reveals cognitive and emotional problems like depression or anxiety that are affecting the learning process, detailed recommendations will be discussed with you and your family, if you want them to participate in the exit session. You will also be given a letter for your school requesting special accommodations if needed. This letter will list detailed recommendations such as more time to complete exams and assignments, fewer classes, tutoring, obtaining a note taker, using visual aids, or other academic adjustments and auxiliary aids. Federal law dictates that schools receiving government funding—which means state colleges and universities and almost all others—must offer such accommodations and follow the neuropsychologist's recommendations to help you pass classes and graduate. If emotional problems are affecting school performance in addition to cognitive ones, you need to consider therapy and possibly see a psychiatrist to discuss the benefit of medications.

Similar problems may be seen in high school students, especially at a college preparatory school that requires more homework and learning of a lot of new material in relatively short periods of time. In any case, the neuropsychological evaluation can help identify specific cognitive and emotional problems and provide detailed recommendations. High school students are also given letters asking for special accommodations, so parents who are thinking about taking their child out of a preparatory school should find a neuropsychologist and have the child evaluated.

However, for a high school student who suddenly starts failing, the first thing parents need to do is make sure no street drugs are involved. I suggest getting a student in this situation into counseling and working with the therapist to identify the source of the problem. If street drugs aren't involved and the child isn't fatigued from lack of sleep, he or she needs to be seen by a primary care physician for a comprehensive physical exam that includes lab tests to rule out medical reasons for the problems. If no such problems are found, psychiatric problems may have to be ruled out, especially if the child is depressed or becomes very moody or angry. However, significant mood changes, including anger outbursts, may also be a sign of street drug use.

If your child is already in counseling, the counselor may suggest seeing a psychiatrist for medication evaluation. A neuropsychological evaluation can help if there is no progress in treatment or no clear etiology, which means we still don't know what is causing the problems. I'm not saying that neuropsychological evaluation will be the answer to all questions. Life is more complex than science can solve, but it can help identify problems and put your child on track for solving them.

I need to mention here that in rare cases, failing school and overall difficulty functioning in the upper years of high school or the college years may result from the onset of severe mental illness, such as bipolar disorder, schizophrenia, or severe depression, especially if the student is far away from her or his family. The stress of dealing with the demands of school as well as planning and organizing everyday life which was previously done by parents can be overwhelming for some young people. Sometimes prolonged severe stress can trigger the onset of mental illness, but I have to emphasize again that these are rare cases. I've had only a few in thirty years of practice. However, if there is a history of mental illness in the family, I wouldn't wait but would try to get the student psychiatric help as soon as possible.

~9~
How Neuropsychological Evaluation Can Help If You Have Difficulty Completing Your Duties at Work

UNDIAGNOSED COGNITIVE PROBLEMS MAY PLAY A MAJOR role in a work situation. This is frequently seen when a person is promoted to a new position or is starting a different job that requires more duties or completion of a new variety of duties in a shorter time period. In your previous position, you were able to get by or even excel, but now you're finding yourself having difficulty or feeling completely lost. Do not panic. Get evaluated!

* * *

Helen was a thirty-eight-year-old woman with a college degree in business who was referred to us by her physician. She had recently been promoted to a supervisory position and found herself having difficulty completing her work duties. She said she was making stupid mistakes and was afraid that her superiors saw them. She had more meetings to attend than before and found herself spacing out and missing important information. She had difficulty finishing tasks and prioritizing. She felt that she needed to complete too many tasks at the same time. As a result, she had unfinished tasks and was getting behind on deadlines. All of those problems made her feel stressed and overwhelmed, and she was afraid she might lose her job. She wondered if something was wrong with her brain.

I explained to her what kind of testing we would do to address her concerns. Afterward, it turned out that she had undiagnosed ADHD and some anxiety. She was referred for therapy and medication evaluation, and was told to call back if she had further concerns. She called several weeks later, thanking me and saying she had learned to manage her problems and was doing better.

The neuropsychological evaluation will help you find out about your cognitive strengths and weaknesses and help you deal with problems. The evaluation is completely confidential, and neither your boss nor coworkers will know about it or have access to the records unless you tell them or show them the report. Not even your family will know unless you want them to have that information.

If you're having difficulty at work and need accommodations, then after the evaluation is completed, I can provide a short letter asking for specific accommodations for you. Your workplace doesn't need a lot of information about your cognitive and mental conditions. It needs to know only what accommodations you'll require, which is required under the Americans with Disabilities Act. Most workplaces, especially federal or state facilities, are accommodating.

However, the work situation for a person who suffers from TBI or stroke is a completely different story. If the TBI or stroke was severe, it is possible that the person cannot return to work and will need to be placed on disability. If the person has enough years of work experience, an application for Social Security Disability Insurance (SSDI) can be submitted. This is designed for people who become disabled before retirement age. You can find more information on the SSDI web page or by talking to a disability lawyer. Some offer a free initial consultation.

If you're not sure if you can return to work, or have returned and found that you cannot perform as well as before, you should be referred for a neuropsychological evaluation. This will show your strengths and weaknesses, and the neuropsychologist will make recommendations, but it's your decision whether to follow them.

However, in cases where your work has a significant safety component, such as if you were an air traffic controller, you won't be able to return to work without an official release from the physician who referred you for the evaluation. Your physician will study the neuropsychologist's recommendations and make an informed decision.

~10~
How Neuropsychological Evaluation Can Help Your Primary Care Physician, Neurologist, Psychiatrist, and Other Medical Care Providers

THE MAIN PURPOSE OF THE NEUROPSYCHOLOGICAL EVALuation is to enable you, the patient, to understand how your brain is working and what you can do to make it better. The other important purpose involves your treatment providers: physicians and therapists. (I'll talk about therapists in the next chapter.) It's important to understand that neuropsychological evaluation is a form of consultation done for your referring physician, nurse practitioner, therapist, case manager, care coordinator, etc., so that this person can better understand your conditions and provide more-suitable treatment. A neuropsychologist usually does not provide treatment.

Most referrals come from neurologists, psychiatrists, and primary care physicians who are familiar with the work of neuropsychologists and appreciate the therapeutic input of the neuropsychological evaluation. However, other medical specialists, such as immunologists, oncologists, hematologists, and pediatricians, have found that the evaluation helps in their work with patients.

The main purpose of the evaluation for your treatment providers is to guide them in planning and implementing the most suitable treatment for you, since every patient is different and requires an individualized therapeutic approach. What is even more important, most diseases don't have a typical handbook presentation, and the more diagnostic information physicians can have, the better their treatment approach will be.

In my practice, I frequently hear, "Please give me some help with this patient, any help you can give me." The truth is that nobody knows everything, no matter how long she or he practices or how many degrees the practitioner has. Life and our bodies are much more complicated than what can be found in textbooks. Therefore, everybody in the health care field needs friendly professionals who can be trusted to brainstorm with about complex cases. This type of consultation seeks to get helpful ideas or find out if the professional is on the right track with the patient: Am I thinking and testing appropriately and not missing anything that can be important in the process? Since most cases referred to neuropsychologists are quite complex, I greatly appreciate the fact that physicians are asking questions and want more information to make more-informed treatment decisions.

If you've been experiencing cognitive problems:
Frequently, referral questions from physicians or other primary care providers involve problems with memory and thinking. Some patients go to the physician's office because they just don't feel right. They think something is going on but aren't sure what it is. Often, they think they may have memory problems.

It's important to emphasize that *memory complaints aren't necessarily memory problems*. You may think you have memory problems because you have difficulty remembering what you've been doing or what people are telling you. In fact, these may be due to problems with your attention, executive functioning, information processing, anxiety, depression, etc. All of the above can make you feel forgetful, but they aren't necessarily memory problems, and require different therapeutic approaches. For example, if you have difficulty paying attention to what you're doing or what people are telling you, you won't remember the conversation you had with a person, especially if you have a habit of multitasking most of the time. Your brain may have never registered it.

I always tell patients that what you did not put into your brain cannot be taken out, so there's no point in arguing with your spouse over whether you were told something. You probably didn't pay attention when she was talking. The neuropsychological evaluation will identify the problems you're having and help you find the most effective solutions.

In cases of head trauma, stroke, or other neurological problems or diseases:

A significant number of physicians' referrals are related to concussions, TBIs resulting from car accidents or falls, sports-related head trauma, transient ischemic attacks, and strokes or other neurological problems or diseases. If you had one of these problems even several years ago and were never evaluated, it's still a good idea to contact a neuropsychologist. You usually don't need a formal referral, but if you do have a referring physician, that doctor needs to know about your current level of functioning after the neurological event, as well as your cognitive strengths and weaknesses. The main questions to answer are how your current difficulties affect your everyday life, your family functioning, and your work situation. Your medical provider needs to know if you'll require additional services for recovery, such as therapy, in-home services, community services, or case management. The physician also needs to know if you have emotional problems such as depression, mood problems, or anxiety that are affecting your functioning, and how much they're affecting your functioning. Depression and anxiety do not facilitate healing. An evaluation of your emotional problems can lead to effective treatment.

If you or a family member suffers from physical problems or chronic pain or disease:

Another referral question may involve chronic pain or chronic systemic illnesses such as multiple sclerosis, cancer, debilitating arthritis, etc. Chronic pain and any chronic and systemic illness can affect the way your brain is functioning, especially if you're taking pain medications such as oxycodone, Percocet, or OxyContin daily for an extended period of time. These are all powerful synthetic narcotics and affect your cognitive and emotional functioning. My chronic pain patients on these medications frequently complain about difficulty thinking, memory problems, and, most of all, about "brain fog" that affects their everyday life and work performance. Eventually, some of them are unable to work and need to apply for disability benefits. In the case of patients with chronic pain and chronic systemic diseases, the evaluation will help identify cognitive and emotional problems and provide treatment recommendations for the patient and family. It is important to recognize that any chronic disease affects the entire family. Recent research suggests that chronic use of medications prescribed for anxiety, such as benzodiazepines and some sleep medications, are linked to memory problems and to progressive cognitive decline such as dementia. It is well researched that anxiety can be successfully treated with therapy. So if you're suffering from anxiety, instead of pumping benzodiazepine pills, which are highly addictive, please make an appointment with a therapist who specializes in anxiety disorders and start treatment. If you've made satisfactory progress in the treatment of anxiety and still have cognitive problems, such as difficulty in processing information or focusing, then it's time to schedule an appointment with a neuropsychologist.

In case of chronic or acute mental illness:

The neuropsychological evaluation also helps when referral questions are related to chronic or acute mental illness. If you or a family member has a history of mental illness or has suffered from an acute episode of mental illness involving visual or auditory hallucinations or paranoid ideation, your physician and therapist need to know your level of functioning. They'll also want to know how effectively you can process information and if you have memory or other cognitive problems that will affect your treatment progress and recovery.

If your family member is suffering from chronic and severe mental illness such as schizophrenia, then there may be some cognitive decline with age. This usually results from the combined effect of the illness itself and factors such as homelessness, street drug abuse, poor access to care, and treatment noncompliance. It may also be associated with use of a variety of psychotropic medications for many years. Such medications are necessary in the case of chronic mental illness, but they do have side effects, and some of these affect cognition.

We still don't know for sure what causes schizophrenia and other severe mental illnesses, but science has made great progress, and current medications have fewer debilitating side effects for the patient's overall functioning than the older generation of psychotropic medications. Chronic use of the older generation of antipsychotic medications was associated with akathisia, which is a permanent movement disorder that is difficult to treat.

Chronic mental illness usually is associated with some kind of cognitive decline, sometimes of a progressive nature. However, this varies, as everything in life usually does. Therefore, some chronic mentally ill patients may have a significant cognitive decline, others may have reasonably good cognitive functioning, and some may have very good cognitive functioning. The prime example of the latter is Winston Churchill, who reportedly suffered from bipolar disorder and treated it with a bottle of bourbon a day, leading to the condition's not seeming to affect his ability to be an exceptional British prime minister during the difficult time of World War II. Another example is Ted Turner, founder of CNN. He reportedly has been taking lithium, the main medication for bipolar disorder, most of his life. And Michelangelo, the Renaissance genius, reportedly also suffered from bipolar disorder.

Some chronically mentally ill patients can be quite impaired and require a treatment guardian or plenary guardian. The former is appointed by the court to make treatment decisions for a patient. The latter is also appointed by a court for this purpose but additionally to make other decisions such as those involving medical care, living situation, and financial affairs. The court-appointed guardian may be a family member, family lawyer, or a corporate guardian who works for a guardianship company.

To decide on petitioning the court to appoint a guardian, a competency evaluation must be completed. This is frequently done by a neuropsychologist and needs to answer questions about whether the patient has sufficient capacity to make fully informed decisions regarding his or her living situation, financial affairs, and medical care. Such an evaluation is also done in cases of progressive neurocognitive diseases such as dementia, and for neurodevelopmental disorders such as intellectual disability (previously known as mental retardation). The neuropsychological evaluation will help a physician and other care providers determine what level of care a patient needs. For example, can the patient safely live independently in the community? Can the patient remain at home with the help of a few hours of home health care? Or does the patient need to be in a group home or nursing home with 24/7 care? These are complex questions and require in-depth and comprehensive neuropsychological evaluation.

In the case of major neurocognitive disorders (also known as dementia, such as Alzheimer's dementia):
Much of an adult neuropsychology practice is related to evaluations for major neurocognitive disorders (dementia). This is one of the most difficult and time-consuming evaluations because it requires a very comprehensive art-and-science approach. Hardly ever, especially in the early stage of dementia, is the clinical picture consistent with the handbook description of this brain disease. Frequently, the neuropsychologist needs to spend time searching the literature and consulting with colleagues. In addition, it may be necessary to read many clinical records and analyze the neuropsychological data. An enormous responsibility is involved in giving the diagnosis of dementia because of the end-of-life trauma related to the disease.

All forms of dementia are progressive and debilitating. Therefore, the diagnostic process needs to be done responsibly and respectfully. Imagine yourself having been given the diagnosis of dementia if it turned out that the situation could be remediated. This could occur because of such disorders as normal pressure hydrocephalus, undiagnosed anemia due to internal bleeding, or other neurological conditions that can mimic early-stage dementia but really are benign brain tumors.

* * *

In my practice, I've had a few unfortunate cases of patients who were referred to me after being incorrectly diagnosed with dementia. I especially remember the case of Joseph, a sixty-one-year-old man who was diagnosed with Lewy body dementia, a form of the disease that shares characteristics with both Alzheimer's and Parkinson's disease. Since this disease, like all forms of dementia, causes progressive cognitive decline, the unfortunate patient spent several months getting his affairs together. He was preparing for the final period of his life, in which he expected to be incapacitated. I can only imagine how traumatic it was for him and his family.

But as time progressed, he noticed that rather than getting worse, he was becoming somewhat better cognitively. He called our office asking for a second opinion. Test results indeed showed improvement since his previous evaluation, and his overall clinical presentation was not consistent with dementia. However, the man did suffer from severe depression. He was referred to his primary care physician for a comprehensive physical exam, and was diagnosed with normal pressure hydrocephalus, which is a treatable condition. He recovered quite well and was able to resume normal functioning.

* * *

Alfredo was a seventy-five-year-old retired art teacher and artist. He was a real gentleman, neatly dressed, with great manners and sweetness in his demeanor. He was brought to my office by his wife since he had stopped driving a few weeks previously after hitting a fence when returning from the library. He told me later that he simply hadn't seen the fence. His wife said he had been diagnosed with early dementia and had stopped painting, would just sit in his studio, was very depressed and fatigued, and took several naps during the day. It was difficult for her to see him fading away, and she wanted to know if anything could be done for him or if she could do anything to help him feel better.

Intrigued by this case, I agreed to do the evaluation. Working with this intelligent and creative person was a great pleasure. When the evaluation was completed, it turned out that he was still very bright. He had some cognitive deficits and severe depression, but his overall clinical presentation was not consistent with early-stage dementia. I had a feeling something physical was going on with him, and referred him to his physician for a comprehensive in-depth physical exam.

Sadly, this case did not have a happy ending. His wife told us that a couple of weeks after the evaluation, her husband collapsed at home and passed away in a hospital from internal bleeding. This case haunted me for a long time because I believe that his life could have been saved if his severe anemia had been found and he had not been misdiagnosed with dementia.

Evaluations for dementia usually are quite traumatic for both the patient and the examining neuropsychologist. There is no good way to tell the patient or family that she or he is suffering from such a progressive and debilitating disease. Frequently, several people are in the room during the exit session: the patient, spouse, and adult children, with the family all crying and the neuropsychologist trying to emotionally "hold the room." This is always quite exhausting, and after I get home, I have only enough energy to get to the tub for a refreshing and rejuvenating bath.

The exit session can be quite long, more than an hour or an hour and a half, especially if the family is large and everybody wants questions answered. Therefore, I schedule it at the end of the day so I don't have to stress about time and can give the patient and family my undivided attention.

Part of the trauma of dementia is that there is still no cure, although medicines on the market may slow its progression. Not all the family's questions can be answered, especially regarding the etiology, since we still don't know what causes dementia, though there are several theories.

Alzheimer's accounts for about 80 percent of dementias in the elderly, and one theory holds that it is caused by tangles and tau protein in the brain. However, the 90+ Study in which the University of California at Irvine looked at people who were ninety or older (Kawas, C. H. et al. 2015; Corrada, M. M. et al. 2016) found tangles and tau proteins in the brains of people who died and did not have any form of dementia, and there were no tangles and tau protein in the brains of some people who died with the diagnosis of dementia. Some of those with dementia, however, had multiple "micro-strokes" that affected blood supply to the brain.

Most referrals for neuropsychological evaluation come from physicians' offices. If you are a self-referral, it may be a good idea to send a copy of the report to your physician. This is a decision that you need to make, but you can talk about it with the neuropsychologist at the exit session when your test results and recommendations are discussed. You would have to sign a release of information to your physician, since according to the Health Insurance Portability and Accountability Act (HIPAA) of 1996 and its Final Privacy Rule of 2013, no information can be released to anybody, including family members, without your written permission.

Providing a report to your physician gives him or her a great deal of information about your functioning. For example, a neuropsychologist who notices during the evaluation that your energy level is low and that you haven't seen your physician for a while can recommend that you need a comprehensive physical exam, including testing for thyroid problems or anemia.

~11~
How Neuropsychological Evaluation Can Help Your Therapist

BESIDES COMING FROM PHYSICIANS' OFFICES, REFERRALS for neuropsychological evaluations also come from therapists and from clinical case coordinators of the patient's insurance company. Therapists, and also psychiatrists, at times refer patients whose initial clinical presentation is especially complex, seeking help in clarifying the diagnosis to provide guidance on where and how to start treatment.

Some mental health practitioners say with hesitation when they call our office that they may have a stupid question about the case they are referring. I always say what I learned from a friendly and very experienced psychiatrist: that there are no stupid questions, only sometimes stupid answers.

Therapists usually refer patients who have been in therapy for some time but have made minimal progress or less. This can be frustrating for both the patient and the therapist. The therapist wants to see the "fruits of his labor"—that the patient is getting better. The patient wants to see benefit from the time and money spent attending therapy sessions. Although most insurance companies cover therapy, the patient may have a hefty co-payment. The therapist wants to know if specific cognitive problems may be affecting the therapeutic progress and how to adjust the therapeutic approach to best address the patient's cognitive needs. Difficulty processing information, memory problems, or attention/concentration problems can affect the therapeutic process. Therefore, knowledge about the patient's cognitive problems is an important factor in therapy.

If, for example, neuropsychological evaluation reveals that the patient has short-term memory problems, it may help to have the patient write a short summary of the session afterward with the therapist's help. Written homework or handouts related to the session can be provided. In cases of problems with verbal memory, it can also help for the therapist to use visual aids—even ones as simple as drawing or sketching figures—during sessions.

For patients with memory problems, it can help if therapy sessions occur at least once a week to allow more reinforcement of the therapeutic process. A patient who sees a therapist once a month usually doesn't remember much from the previous session, which makes meaningful progress difficult.

Some patients have problems with attention/concentration. The neuropsychological evaluation will help determine if a person has ADHD, what kind of ADHD, and how the patient can be helped. Once the diagnosis is made, specific recommendations need to be included in the neuropsychological evaluation report.

Another important factor that affects therapeutic progress is related to difficulty processing information or with verbal comprehension. In my practice, this is often an issue with patients whose overall intellectual functioning, and especially verbal abilities, are below average, borderline, or impaired. Difficulty processing information can be seen in some seniors because of hearing issues and slower processing speed. It isn't easy to do in-depth psychotherapy with somebody who cannot engage because hearing is impaired, but it's still important to provide supportive therapy, especially for seniors living alone and without family. This seems to be a growing problem nowadays. The therapist may be the only person the patient sees and talks with on a regular basis who can monitor the patient's mental status. The therapist can call the patient's physician when there's reason for concern.

Generally, for a patient with difficulty processing information, it helps if the therapeutic goals are very specific and there are no more than three at one time. The therapy needs to be down-to-earth and goal-oriented. I frequently advise frustrated therapists that they cannot be too sophisticated with many of these patients, and it may be best to stick to the basics to help them be functional. I advise young and inexperienced therapists to make sure the patient can follow the conversation and fully understands what is being said. To make sure of this, the therapist can ask, "What did you hear me saying?" Also, speaking in shorter sentences with concrete content can help, especially if the patient's intellectual functioning is below average, borderline, or impaired.

~12~
How Neuropsychological Evaluation Can Help Case Managers and Case Coordinators

THIS CHAPTER IS MAINLY FOR THE FAMILIES OF PATIENTS who need case management services—those who are developmentally disabled, suffer from chronic and severe mental illness, or are disabled as a result of chronic and debilitating medical problems.

Community case managers or case coordinators usually work for large medical or mental health clinics and hospitals, helping patients find the most suitable care and services. Their help is essential for chronically mentally ill and physically and intellectually disabled patients to safely and successfully function in the community. Case management services are mainly available for patients on Medicaid, the government insurance program for people with low income. Unfortunately, most commercial insurance plans don't provide such services, but some of them do provide limited clinical case management.

A case manager who is skillful, knowledgeable about community resources, and dedicated to the community can be a real benefit for the patient and family. For example, such a professional can find a primary care physician, help make appointments with specialists, remind the patient about appointments, and sit with the patient during the appointments, if necessary. Case managers usually don't provide transportation to appointments but are able to arrange this. (In New Mexico, where I practice, all Medicaid patients are eligible for the Safe Ride transportation system.) Case managers can also help with finding community agencies that provide community and home assistance, and sometimes have the authority to approve a higher level of care if necessary.

Case managers who refer a patient for neuropsychological evaluation generally want to know the client's level of functioning. What kind of cognitive problems does the person have, and how much do these problems affect daily functioning? Most important, what community services will be most suitable for the client's needs? The most frequent questions for the neuropsychologist are whether the client can safely live in the community and how many hours of community services per week the client needs. Is in-home assistance needed? Can the client safely take care of hygiene needs? Can the client manage his money or does he need a payee? A payee is a person or institution that manages a client's money and pays his bills. This is an important issue, especially if the patient has poor judgment and poor basic math calculation skills. A disabled person may have $100, spend $90, and believe $50 still is available to pay expenses. Frequently, when the disabled person gets general assistance or disability money, it's spent quickly for nonessential things. Then there isn't enough money to pay rent, and the person can become homeless.

In the case of chronic mental illness, the case manager assists with finding housing or placement in a group home and helps with applying for food stamps and general assistance. Assistance can also be provided in finding agencies in the community that specialize in job training for disabled people or sheltered employment.

The good case manager is a real treasure for a disabled person who doesn't have family support, which is frequently the case with chronically mentally ill people.

~13~
The Exit Session: Discussing the Results of the Evaluation and Recommendations

You've spent several long hours being tested, and you're ready for the results to be presented and explained to you in detail. You also would like to hear detailed recommendations, since you want to know how to improve your brain functioning and generally get better.

Family members are very welcome during the exit session because it's important for them to understand your functional strengths and limitations, and—most important—how they can help you get better. You have to agree in writing and sign a release of information for each family member whom you want to be present at the exit session. If you decide that, for any reason, you don't want to share this information with anybody else, then it will be presented *only* to you. According to HIPAA, a health care provider cannot release clinical information to anybody, even family members, without the patient's written permission. This obviously excludes health emergency situations, but neuropsychologists rarely deal with that.

In summary, *you* are in charge of your clinical information, and it is *your* decision who else is entitled to it. For example, if your spouse, whom you are currently divorcing, calls our office and asks to talk to us, we cannot even provide the information that you've been seen by us. Generally speaking, we want you to feel safe and comfortable during and after the evaluation.

After the exit session, the neuropsychologist will prepare a comprehensive report containing all the recommendations discussed during the exit session. This usually take a couple of weeks but possibly longer if the case is complex and requires literature searches or a consultation with another specialist. Don't worry, your name won't be mentioned. Only specific clinical questions will be discussed.

When the report is ready, you'll be notified, and you can pick it up or it can be mailed to you. The report will also be faxed or mailed to your referral source (usually your physician) and all other health care providers for whom you signed a release form. The report should not be "psychobabble." It should be written in language that you and your treatment providers can easily comprehend. If you don't understand the report's findings or recommendations, you can request a meeting with the neuropsychologist to go over them again.

Now let me go back to the recommendations.

If you find out that despite your worries, your brain is still functioning well, then congratulate yourself, appreciate every day of your life, and seek therapy if you still have worries or depression. Try to do something good for other people. It should make you feel a little better. However, if you have mild or moderate cognitive difficulties, remember the motto of this book: Jon Kabat-Zinn's statement that, "As long as you are breathing, there is more right with you than wrong with you."

Please keep in mind that almost everything is fixable, and you can make your brain work better if you put your heart into it. This means that you need to be motivated and persistent and constantly looking for new ways to help yourself. There is no guarantee in life, but if you focus on improving your brain's functioning, you're increasing the probability that it will get better. In the present information era when you can Google almost everything, it isn't that difficult to find the information you need without spending a lot of time doing research. The neuropsychological evaluation is an individualized clinical process, and every person is different and requires a different therapeutic approach.

Here are some suggestions, exercises, and ideas that I use in my practice which I hope can help inspire you on your journey to a better brain:

If your difficulties are in the area of attention/concentration:

There are several things you can do to improve these skills. A number of medications can offer a quick fix. Most are fast acting without a lot of debilitating side effects. They've been on the market for many years, and most of them are well researched. You don't need to see a psychiatrist for a prescription if a neuropsychological evaluation found that you have attention/concentration problems. Most primary care physicians are now quite knowledgeable in this area and will prescribe medications for you if a neuropsychologist's report says you've been diagnosed with ADHD.

If you're hesitant to take medications, you can start by finding a therapist who specializes in treating ADHD (most of them have a website) and attending therapy on a regular basis until you learn how to cope with your problems. There are several forms of ADHD, and your therapist's individualized treatment may be the best solution. Most health insurance companies cover therapy sessions.

If you cannot attend therapy, you can find attention/concentration exercises on the Internet. Continue doing the ones that help on a regular basis, for perhaps fifteen to thirty minutes a day—in addition to therapy if this is part of your treatment plan. There is also research indicating that specific vitamins and minerals may reduce ADHD symptoms in adults (Rucklidge et al. 2014 and 2017).

I believe that the best remedy for attention/concentration problems is to learn how to meditate and do it daily. Research indicates that meditation can be effective in improving your attention/concentration skills (Mitchell et al. 2017; Herbert, A. and Esparham, A. 2017; Bachmann, K. et al. 2018), possibly as effective as medications (Zylowska et al. 2008, Mitchell et al. 2015). Therefore, if you are committed to helping yourself in this area, go to meditation classes, get a C.D. or a book, or just Google it and practice every day. Consistency is the key.

My patients often say that meditation doesn't help. I try to explain that, like most things in life, it takes practice. If you meditate once or twice a day for five to ten minutes, just following your breath (in and out), with time, it will get much better. This is shown in the movie *Eat Pray Love*, based on the 2006 bestseller by Elizabeth Gilbert. Julia Roberts portrays a woman at a crossroads who is trying to find her true self. A beautiful scene in the film shows her having a lot of difficulty starting a meditation practice in India because her mind is constantly going back to her problems. But persistence and daily practice pay off, and later, you can see that she's able to meditate for a long period of time without distraction.

Many books, C.D.s, and applications are available to teach you how to meditate. I like the smartphone application "10% Happier: Meditation for Fidgety Skeptics," by ABC News correspondent Dan Harris. There's an interesting story behind this application and a 2017 book with the same title.

Another thing that can help improve attention/concentration skills is practicing mindfulness in your everyday life. To be mindful is to be aware of every moment and to pay attention to it because it is unique. The concept was popularized by Jon Kabat-Zinn in the '70s, and has been getting increasing recognition around the world since then (Kabat-Zinn, J., 1994, 2005, 2006).

According to his definition, "Mindfulness means paying attention in a particular way: on purpose, in the present moment, and nonjudgmentally." When he talks about mindfulness in his many TV appearances, he often brings up a powerful illustration. He says something like, if you're in the shower in the morning, just be in the shower, not on your morning meeting at work. He emphasizes that the moment we realize that our mind has drifted away from our present experience and we bring our awareness back to the present moment, we're practicing mindfulness. It's good to do it as much as we can throughout the day. Be aware of the food you eat—its taste and texture—and practice mindful walks. Be aware of the way you walk, how your body is moving, and, most important, be aware of your surroundings. Notice the beauty of nature, and smell the trees, flowers, and wild grasses. After a few minutes, you may feel a beautiful peace in your mind and body when they are in harmony with nature.

I often recommend mindful walks to my patients, since nature is so beautiful in New Mexico. But beautiful and breathtaking places are all over the U.S., and I'm sure there's one close to where you live. If you're an urban person, go to the nearest park for a mindful walk, since it's difficult to practice awareness on busy and noisy streets.

If you have difficulty with executive functioning:
If you have this kind of problem, you aren't good at planning and organizing, and you may have difficulty with effective problem solving, judgment, and insight. Unfortunately, there is no executive functioning pill, so you need to find a therapist or a life coach who knows how to help people with these problems and work diligently with him or her. It'll take a while, since there's no quick fix in this area. Hopefully, with time and treatment, you'll learn how to solve problems more effectively and make fewer impulsive decisions that can have long-term consequences.

Some patients with a history of moderate or severe TBI, which always affects executive functioning such as decision-making and judgment, may need to stay in therapy for many years in order to be safe and functional and avoid getting themselves in trouble. Sadly, throughout my years of clinical practice, I've seen many patients with a history of undiagnosed brain traumas who also have a history of incarceration. All of them had various degrees of impaired executive functioning, in most of them, moderate to severe. I truly believe that if they had received proper treatment after their TBIs, they may have avoided involvement with the legal system. It's much safer and cheaper for society to provide treatment for these individuals than to lock them up, because incarceration only makes them worse.

If in addition to impaired executive functioning, you have emotional problems like anxiety, mood-regulation difficulties, or depression—all or each affecting the ability to function in everyday life—pharmacological intervention might help. You can try therapy first and add medication later. If your depression, anxiety, and mood difficulties improve, it may become easier to solve problems and function better in your everyday life.

Many people who have been diagnosed with ADHD also have executive functioning problems. Therapy and ADHD medications can help in such cases, simply because you will be more organized and better able to pay attention to what you're doing. Smartphone applications are available that will help with organization. Your phone will remind you about daily and weekly tasks that need to be completed.

If you have problems with memory:
It's important to realize that *memory complaints aren't necessarily memory problems.* You may think you have memory problems but in fact, have problems with attention, anxiety, depression, PTSD, chronic fatigue, complex medical problems, etc. All of these, and many other factors, can cause difficulty remembering. You need to be evaluated to find out if you truly have memory problems.

If you have difficulty remembering because of any of the above factors, you need to deal with them. Then, your memory and possibly other cognitive problems may improve. Depression, mood problems, PTSD, and anxiety, separately or together, can affect memory functioning.

It's good to start with individual therapy and add medication management if needed. Most therapists treat depression and anxiety, since they're so common. Some therapists specialize in PTSD, mood disorders, chronic medical problems, chronic pain, etc. The website of your state psychologists or counselors association will list these practitioners and tell what kind of problems they treat and what insurance plans they take.

It needs to be emphasized that most chronic medical problems and most systemic diseases such as cancer will cause at least temporary short-term memory problems. In the case of cancer, chemotherapy can cause memory and other cognitive problems that may get better after the treatment. Anemias, thyroid dysfunction, chronic fatigue, and immunological and neurological disorders all may cause memory problems. An evaluation will help you understand if you truly have memory problems as opposed to merely memory complaints, and what kind of memory problems you have. Memory is a complex cognitive function.

Here are some tips to get you started on the journey into better brain health. It's worth noting that *all* cognitive exercises are good for maintaining cognitive functioning. Maintaining relatively good cognitive functioning to the end of life lets people take care of themselves and not be a burden to their families.

If neuropsychological evaluation reveals that you have difficulty with verbal memory, there are many ways to improve this. Computer games are available, including ones free to members on the AARP website. You can also watch the *Brain Games* show on TV. If you're serious about improving your verbal memory, it would be good to read a short story daily and then try to write down what you remember from it. If you don't remember much, read it again but divide it into two or three parts. Your brain makes connections between neurons, which are brain cells that carry information, almost to the end of your life. Therefore, if you diligently work on improving and maintaining your brain function, it probably will serve you well to the end of your days.

If you have verbal retrieval problem, which means you're frequently searching for words, it can help to play any kind of word game you enjoy. In addition, writing down a word you've forgotten once you recall it and then trying to make associations will help pull the word from your memory the next time you need it. This "mnemonic strategy" may include organizing items into meaningful groups and using imagery or visualization. It also can help if you take the time to find out which kinds of associations are easier for you to make. This may be a color, shape, sound, or another easier word. For example, if you have a tendency to forget the name of the street your friend lives on—let's say Browning—you can associate it with the color brown, a name, or a short sentence. For example, "Mike Brown lives on Browning Street." You can also use shapes to help you remember numbers, such as "egg" for zero and "chair" for the number four. Use your creativity.

If you have difficulty with nonverbal memory and or visual-spatial memory, you need to concentrate on cognitive exercises that involve pictures, shapes, colors, spatial relations, etc. Once again, computer games are a good source. And the coloring books for adults that are now in fashion, although their primary goal is providing calmness in a busy life, can also be a source of visual memory training if you try to visualize what you've just colored.

If you have difficulty with fine motor skills, there are a lot of things you can do to improve them. One of most helpful and creative ways can be working with beads. Maybe it will also become your hobby or passion, and you can even earn money making jewelry from different kinds of beads. You can ask your physician for a consultation with an occupational therapist who will evaluate your visual-spatial skills and fine motor skills and give you exercises to do at home, preferably daily.

Sometimes patients ask me what cognitive exercise will be the best for them. The answer is quite simple: the one you are doing. Anything you do regularly to improve your brain functioning will help you improve or maintain cognitive functioning. Any kind of brain stimulation is better than sitting and worrying that you're not getting better. Even daily walking is a good brain exercise. So get up and do something that will bring you joy and pleasure, since that will be most beneficial for your brain.

However, if you have multiple cognitive difficulties, it usually means that medical problems are affecting your brain/body functioning. Your brain doesn't work in isolation; everything going on in your body will affect on it. The first thing to do is make an appointment with your primary care physician for a comprehensive physical exam and get laboratory tests, including brain studies. These will help find out if there's a medical reason for your problems. A huge variety of factors may result in your brain's not working to the best of its ability. You need to find out what these factors are. Keep in mind that every brain is different, and different combinations of factors may have to be considered in your particular case.

If you have emotional in addition to cognitive problems:

If you have emotional problems in addition to cognitive ones, you're not alone. Most people with cognitive difficulties also have problems such as anxiety, sadness, depression, or sleep issues. It doesn't have to be full-blown anxiety or depression, but you may have some symptoms. Usually, if you notice cognitive issues, it may take time to find the right specialist and the right diagnosis. Meanwhile, you may have fears, worries, and sleepless nights.

If, indeed, the neuropsychological evaluation confirms that your cognitive problems are mild and you still have emotional problems, I suggest finding a therapist who specializes in anxiety and depression, even if you only have symptoms rather than a clinical diagnosis, and start attending therapy sessions. If you sign a release of information, the therapist will get your neuropsychological evaluation report, which will help in finding the most suitable treatment. The therapist may also work on improving your cognitive problems.

It will help if you have three to five specific treatment goals, all with a time frame. You need a clear understanding of what you want to achieve in that time. If you have difficulty making progress on your goals, they will need to be modified to address your cognitive and emotional state. Do *not* get discouraged and give up on yourself. Remember the old sayings, "It always seems impossible until it's done," and "Yesterday's errors are today's power."

Make sure you write down how you want to reward yourself when you reach your goals, since this can be a very important motivational factor. It can be anything from a small treat like ice cream to something bigger such as traveling. You can get creative here.

It's important to treat your emotional problems promptly because depression, anxiety, and sleep issues do not facilitate healing. Most people do have fears, but their fears don't have to have *them*, and that's what makes the difference. The same with sadness and depressive thoughts. Your therapist will be working on helping you reach your emotional goals, but you need patience, since every treatment takes time. If your anxiety and depression get better but you still have sleep problems, your primary care physician may need to refer you for a sleep study. This can determine if there are medical reasons for your difficulties, such as apnea or other sleep disorders.

If you or a loved one suffered a TBI, stroke, or other neurological problems, that's a totally different situation. Changes resulting from brain traumas, even mild ones, and other neurological diseases affect mood regulation and usually cause behavioral problems, frequently in addition to anxiety and depressive symptoms. This results from an injury to the frontal lobes, especially in the subcortical areas, which are responsible for controlling mood and behavior. These lobes act like brakes in the brain, and if they're not working properly, a person has significant difficulty controlling mood and behavior. Injury to this area may result in frequent mood changes, anger outbursts, and rage.

If mood dysregulation is severe and you start exhibiting psychotic symptoms such as paranoid ideation or hallucinations, it's time to see a psychiatrist for medication evaluation. This needs to be done in addition to attending therapy on a regular basis, because medications don't talk and won't teach you how to cope with your problems.

Sometimes behavioral therapy, which is done by a behavioral modification specialist, may help. This is especially indicated with behaviorally challenged patients who also suffer from a speech disorder such as aphasia, where talk therapy may be difficult. Many patients with dementia have a broad array of emotional, behavioral, and psychotic symptoms. If the dementia is advanced, therapy isn't very effective and psychotropic medications may be the only choice, especially if the patient becomes out of control or violent. Controlling these symptoms is important for the safety of the patient and his or her social environment.

~14~
Mastering Your Strengths

NEUROPSYCHOLOGICAL EVALUATION NOT ONLY TELLS YOU what cognitive difficulties you're having and their severity (mild, moderate, or severe) but, most importantly, it will tell you what your cognitive strengths are. Obviously, you can use your strengths to help overcome your weaknesses, or at least make them less problematic in your daily life.

I encourage my patients to work on mastering their strengths to incorporate them into their daily life and their work/careers. This is most important for high school students, young adults, or people who want to change careers. I encourage them to take the Clifton StrengthsFinder Test, also called Gallup Strengths Test, which is an online psychological assessment of personal strengths and the unique and natural talents we were born with. I'm not crazy about online psychological assessments, but I truly recommend this one because it is valid, reliable, practical, and eye opening for many people. You may find that you have talents you never thought you had. You can take it by going to www.gallupstrengthscenter. com; it will be money well spent. The test gives you a more in-depth self-understanding and helps you make plans based on your unique talents. (I have to emphasize that I am not in any way associated with the Gallup organization and have no financial incentives related to this test.)

The strengths assessment was developed by the Gallup Institute under the leadership of a psychologist, Dr. Donald Clifton (1924–2003). The positive psychology movement that he was part of emphasizes optimal human functioning. It took him and his coworkers half a century to develop the assessment, but it was worth the time. The test precisely measures the presence of talents in thirty-four general areas referred to as "themes." For about $20, you can find out what your five signature themes (talents) are in rank order. You can purchase an assessment of all thirty-four natural talents for an additional fee, but knowing the first five will be the most informative and practical. The assessment also comes with action-planning tools for your talents—practical recommendations on how to develop them and make your talents work more effectively.

For additional money, you can also get help from a personal coach to better understand and develop your talents. Try it.

~15~
How to Deal with a Loved One Who Has "Brain Problems"

PATIENTS WHO HAVE PROBLEMS RELATED TO BRAIN FUNCtioning need a somewhat different approach by their loved ones, whether the problems are mild, such as temporary ones after mild brain trauma or transient ischemic attack, or more major, like those that occur after a stroke, tumor, or mild to moderate dementia. Here are some ideas that have worked for patients and their loved ones based on my experience in more than thirty years of clinical work.

Most important are problems related to processing verbal information and memory, because they affect verbal comprehension, communication with family members, everyday functioning, and all social interactions. Of course, it's difficult to change your way of communicating with your loved ones from day to day, but with practice, it will get better. The goal is to make sure that communication is ongoing, which will tremendously help the relationship between your loved one and the extended family. Your loved one is already going through the difficult process of finding a new normal, and you need to facilitate that process as much as possible. You both will have good days and bad days, but don't get discouraged and don't give up on keeping the communication going, despite difficulties. Do *not* feel guilty if you aren't getting your point across and your loved one becomes irritable. The situation will get better with practice.

If you feel that you've "hit the wall," try to find professional help. Make an appointment with a therapist and discuss your difficulties. Taking time to take care of your feelings is important for your own peace of mind and for the relationship. If you're lucky, your loved one will agree to counseling. If not and he or she gets angry about it or starts to make degrading comments, please remember that the patient's ability to reason may be compromised. So go ahead and go by yourself because you need guidance and support, especially in the case of progressive decline of overall functioning, such as dementia.

Here are some recommendations: Try to speak slowly to your love one and in short sentences. Don't try to tell her or him everything at once. For example, don't tell the whole long story of what happened to the neighbor's dog. The person listening will probably get lost in the middle of the telling. If you see that happening, start again, but make your tale simple and to the point.

If you need to discuss some important issue, make sure that he or she understands it properly. If it feels like the listener is lost, ask, "What did you hear me saying?" If it wasn't what you meant, than repeat it slowly and use an example.

Don't argue or try to get your point across several times if your loved one doesn't understand. Unfortunately, with more advanced brain problems, reasoning may be compromised. There's no point trying to reason with somebody whose reasoning ability is compromised. It will only make the other person irritable or agitated, which may cause more problems. Also, please remember that anxiety, depression, and agitation do not facilitate healing. A peaceful environment helps everybody in the family. However, life is life, and peacefulness may not always be possible. Just keep in mind what your goal is, and don't feel guilty if you've had a bad day. Remember, "Tomorrow is another day," as Scarlett O'Hara used to say in *Gone with the Wind*.

At some point, written communication may help, especially if the loved one has problems with executive functioning. If you want her or him to do some chores around the house or go shopping, make a list or a step-by-step flowchart. This also helps for people who have difficulty starting projects.

Remember that the brain functions less efficiently after any kind of trauma, and can't take too much at once. If too much is going on, your loved one can suddenly become agitated. Don't plan long or tiring trips, or doing too much in the same day. Make sure there's time to rest. Plan doctor visits and other important meetings or family gatherings in the morning, with only one visit or event per day if possible. With dementia and some brain traumas, a well-known phenomenon called "sundown syndrome" occurs: Simply stated, when the sun goes down, brain functioning also does, becoming much less efficient. Keeping that in mind will make your life much easier.

A general rule is that the brain heals better and faster in people who are emotionally well, optimistic about the future, and believe they can overcome their problems. Let your loved one enjoy life the way he or she wants if it isn't harmful and the social environment is comfortable. Try not to add a lot of restrictions all at once, believing that it will speed recovery. It may not, but loving support and patience will always pay off. Happiness is better than any kind of pill. The extra little piece of chocolate, at times, can make a person a little happier. We're only in this world for a while, so why not make it nicer if we can?

~16~
Menopause and Memory

MEMORY AND OTHER COGNITIVE PROBLEMS EXPERIENCED by women during menopause are real and appear to be more acute in the first year after the final menstrual period (Weber, M. T. et al. 2013). The changes in hormones and natural decline of estrogen affect all women's bodies, including their brains. Learning and memory are associated with those regions of the brain (hippocampus and prefrontal cortex) that are rich in estrogen receptors. Women may complain of "fuzzy thinking" (Northrup, C. 2002) or "cotton head," an inability to think straight, organizational problems, attention/concentration difficulties, mood swings, and depression. These commonly are not symptoms of dementia, and memory usually returns to what is normal for the person's age. However, about 5 percent of women older than sixty have some form of dementia, and the percentage increases as you age; after seventy, it's 12 percent. I strongly agree with Dr. Northrup, who said, "Women need to know that statistical data on dementia cannot predict whether any particular woman will develop memory problems." (Northrup 2002, p. 566).

* * *

Janet was a fifty-three-year-old nurse, tall and elegantly dressed, who was referred to me by her physician. Visibly anxious, she stated with tearful eyes and trembling voice: "I may have the beginning of dementia." When asked detailed questions about her problems, she said she had been forgetful for the past few months and was making stupid mistakes at work. She had no family history of dementia, but her best friend's husband had been recently diagnosed with early-stage Alzheimer's. She had noticed him having memory problems, and was afraid she could be experiencing similar problems as well.

After talking for a while to make her more comfortable, I explained that memory complaints aren't necessarily memory problems, and told her what kind of testing we would be doing. I mentioned that most patients with dementia have problems with judgment and insight, and tend to be in denial about their memory and other cognitive problems. Most of them are brought for evaluation by family members who see changes in their functioning that are not obvious to the patients themselves.

This made Janet feel more comfortable and eager to start testing. She mentioned that she had been menopausal for the past year and wondered if that might have something to do with her cognitive functioning difficulty.

Testing found that her memory was generally within the normal range for her age, and her verbal memory was above that range. She exhaled with relief. I explained that some menopausal women experience memory and cognitive problems, especially in the first year, but that it usually comes back to normal. Therefore, Janet's memory may have been somewhat higher before menopause, but at present, there was no reason for her to worry. She was advised that we had good baseline results for her memory functioning, and she could return for retesting if she had concerns in the future. She might also benefit from therapy to help her deal with anxiety and stress at work. She called several weeks later thanking me and telling me she was doing much better.

Janet's story isn't that uncommon. In my clinical practice, I see several middle-aged women a year who are experiencing memory problems and are afraid they're having the beginnings of dementia. The fear of losing their mind and being unable to function causes them sadness, depression, and insomnia, and significantly affects their quality of life. So if you experience this problem, instead of dwelling on the unknown, talk with your physician or other health care provider about whether you can benefit from a neuropsychological evaluation. The memory tests have specific norms for every age. They will help find out if, in fact, you have memory problems or merely memory complaints, and if you have problems, what kind they are, verbal or visual, or which memory processes, retentive memory or encoding, are affected. This specific information will allow the neuropsychologist to give you detailed information as to what you can do to improve your overall functioning and the quality of your life.

* * *

Please remember this: Most of the time, you can improve your brain functioning, even after a major neurological event or illness.

You simply need to find the best and most effective way of doing it with the help of your health care professionals. Take the example of Dr. Jill Bolte Taylor, a neuroscientist who recovered quite well after a massive stroke and wrote a fascinating book, *My Stroke of Insight: A Brain Scientist's Personal Journey* (2008).

~17~
How to Find a Neuropsychologist

NEUROPSYCHOLOGISTS ARE A RARE BREED, BUT IF YOU'RE lucky, your physician or therapist will have a working relationship with one. You can also call your insurance company and ask for a list of contracted neuropsychologists in your area, or you can go to your state psychological association website. Most of them have a "Find a Psychologist" page where you can also find a neuropsychologist who is licensed in your state. Some neuropsychologists have websites describing the scope of their practice. A formal referral from your medical provider isn't usually required. Just call the neuropsychologist's office, ask any questions you have, and make an appointment.

The process is quite a different story, though, if you have straight Medicare rather than a Medicare-managed care plan. Medicare requires a written referral from a physician or other medical provider, such as a physician assistant or nurse practitioner, so if this applies to you, a written referral is needed when you come for the first appointment. The referral doesn't have to be an elaborate letter, only a couple of sentences saying that you're being referred and giving the reason.

A neuropsychological evaluation is considered a medical benefit by most insurance plans and is covered, but some insurance companies require pre-authorization. This means that after the initial intake session, the neuropsychologist sends specific clinical forms to the insurance company for approval of the time needed for evaluation.

Part II
Brain Health

~18~
The Power of Proper Nutrition

MANY HEALTH CARE PROFESSIONALS, MYSELF INCLUDED, believe that *food is our medicine*, which is why we must consider nutrition in any discussion of our health.

As mentioned before, your brain is a miraculous part of your body. Much contemporary research proves that brain functioning can be improved at any age and in most circumstances if done in the right way. Proper nutrition is essential for your body, brain, and well-being. We know now that our gut produces 90 percent of serotonin, the "feel good" substance in your brain, much more than your brain produces. That's why it's sometimes called "the second brain." Your gut's health is also essential for your immune system. Therefore, brain health needs to start with gut health.

The importance of probiotics and prebiotics (fermented food):

Your gut health depends on the amount and diversity of "good bacteria," which are essential for the proper working of your intestines and the entire body. Good bacteria in our gut fights the "bad bacteria" there so we can stay healthy. When

Jars of home-made prebiotics (pickled beets and pickled red cabbage). Instructions on how to make them are included in this chapter.

Jar of home-made dill pickles. Instructions on how to make them are included in this chapter.

we age or have medical problems, especially if we take antibiotics, the amount of good bacteria diminishes and the amount of bad bacteria tends to rise, which can cause more health problems. Therefore, we need to supplement the good bacteria in our intestinal system with probiotics.

As mentioned before, our gut makes much more serotonin than our brain. Therefore, taking probiotics should be part of a daily regimen, not only for the elderly but also for people who struggle with depression, mood problems, or chronic physical problems. You can buy probiotics in every health food store and most groceries. Make sure there is a variety of good bacteria strains in each capsule. As an alternative, you can eat lots of good, possibly organic, yogurt and drink kefir or other drinks with plenty of good bacteria. Remember to always read the label before you buy anything you eat or drink.

In addition to taking probiotics to increase the amount of good bacteria in the gut, we also need to eat prebiotics in fermented food which are the best food for the good bacteria. Prebiotics make the good bacteria healthy and happy, increasing the overall health of the host of the gut, which is you and me. All health food stores now sell fermented foods such as kimchi, sauerkraut, pickled cucumbers, and other vegetables, but pickles are easy to prepare at home for a much lower price and take almost no time. All dietary fiber is good for your gut bacteria. Therefore, remember to eat plenty of greens, vegetables, and legumes.

The easiest and fastest way to make homemade prebiotics such as fermented food is to put your favorite vegetable or a mixture of them in a Mason jar and add equal parts of vinegar and water plus a teaspoon of sea salt. You can use white vinegar or red wine vinegar or half of each for red cabbage and beets, and can add spices and fresh herbs like rosemary, thyme, and onion. Cloves and allspice also go well with beets. Experiment and have fun with it. Cover the jar with a paper towel, put the lid on but don't tighten it, and let it stand on your kitchen counter for about two days. Take the paper towel off and tighten the lid. Put it in the fridge, wait for about two weeks, and then enjoy. Some people say it can stay in the fridge for a month, but I keep it there for two to three months or more, and it's still very good.

I like homemade pickled beets a lot. They're delicious and keep you regular. They have many nutritional values and are low in fat; one cup has only 106 calories. These are a good source of dietary fiber and promote a healthy digestive system and a stable blood sugar level, and also are rich in potassium, magnesium, vitamin A, and good carbohydrates. They can be a good meal after a workout but can be high in sodium if you buy them in the store. In contrast, homemade pickled beets may have only one teaspoon of sodium in the whole small Mason jar, which you usually don't eat in one day since they're quite intense even if you like pickles a lot, as I do. I love to have a few sips of this rich, creamy, and delicious beet brine and a few pieces of pickled beets and onion from the jar right before dinner to keep me regular, but you can also add it to your favorite salads.

I also want to share my favorite dill pickled cucumber recipe, which has been in my family for generations. You need to buy about a pound or more of pickling cucumbers, or you may want to grow your own, which always taste better. Make sure they're not very big, about two to three inches. You also need a few fresh dill branches with the seeds on them. Inspect them for insects and discard the unhealthy-looking ones. Put the branches in the bottom of a big glass or clay jar or a pot. Do *not* use an iron, aluminum, or other metal-based pot. Add a few peeled cloves of garlic, one or two small onions cut into not very small pieces, some pepper, a teaspoon of mustard seeds, and three leaves of horseradish (optional). Wash the cucumbers and crowd them tightly into the jar or pot. Boil a quart of water and let it stand until lukewarm. Add 2.5 tablespoons of salt per liter, stir, and pour into the jar until all the cucumbers are immersed. Then cover with a small ceramic or glass (not paper or plastic) plate facedown, and put a weight on top of the plate.

The fun part is finding a medium-size rock in your backyard, washing it, and using it as a weight on top of the plate. Make sure all the cucumbers are covered by the plate and under the weight. Let the setup stand for about four to five days on the counter or in the pantry. Do *not* put it into the fridge. In about two days, your kitchen will have a healthy and wonderful smell of fresh dill and pickles. All your guests will ask what this earthy smell in the kitchen is. After four to five days, eat and enjoy. They're *delicious*.

If you want to preserve your home-made dill pickles, after they are ready to eat, remove them from the jar or pot and crowd them tightly in Mason jars (usually two or three). Pour in the pickling brine from the original jar or pot until all the cucumbers are immersed. Then put the lids on, tighten them, and place the jars in the fridge. They can be kept there for a few months and still be delicious in the middle of the winter.

The importance of vitamins and supplements:
What does it mean to eat healthy? Most professionals in the area of health and nutrition agree that we need to eat mainly vegetables, some fruits, fish (small fish and freshwater fish because of mercury concerns), and not much red meat (maybe one or two servings per week). And, of course, not many carbohydrates, since they're converted into sugar in our bodies.

However, eating properly isn't enough to keep us healthy in the contemporary world. Pollution and contamination can be found almost everywhere: in the air, soil, water, even in the ocean. Therefore, no matter how clean we try to eat, the food available nowadays is not as healthy as it was a hundred years ago. We need to add vitamins and sometimes other supplements to what we eat, especially if we are elderly or have chronic health conditions.

Most medical professionals would agree that we should take a multivitamin daily. Also very important for our immune system is vitamin D3, which some people are deficient in, especially if they live in northern states with less exposure to sunlight. The level of this vitamin can be checked by a simple blood test. Health care professionals also recommend taking fish oil daily since the omega-3 fatty acids that it contains help reduce inflammation and triglycerides in the body and have other health benefits. Vitamin C is also very important, especially during the cold and flu season.

Information on the internet will tell you that you need a lot of vitamins and supplements to feel healthy and live longer. However, taking a lot of these is not necessary. A primary care physician who is knowledgeable in this area can tell you what your body needs in term of vitamins and supplements. If you're not lucky enough to have such a physician and you're concerned about doing everything you should to remain healthy for a long time, you may find an alternative-medicine physician or other health practitioner who can put you on the most appropriate regimen of vitamins and supplements. This may be a nurse practitioner who specializes in holistic medicine, a naturopath, or a doctor of oriental medicine (DOM). Most DOMs are also knowledgeable in the use of medicinal herbs that may help in some health conditions.

Please don't try to determine your vitamin and supplement regimen by yourself, especially if you have a physical illness and are taking medications, since some vitamins and supplements can interfere with your medications.

The benefits of green tea:
It's important to mention green tea, since this is one of the most powerful antioxidants on the planet. People who drink a lot of it, like the Japanese, have a lower rate of cancer, dementia, and other debilitating diseases. I didn't really like the taste of regular or organic green tea (except sometimes jasmine green tea), and for a long time, just emptied the contents of a tea bag into a smoothie to get its benefit. Then I tasted matcha green tea, the old ceremonial tea unique to Japan. It's the high-

est quality powdered green tea available, made from the nutrient-rich young leaves of the *Camellia sinensis* plant, which grows in the shade.

Made from ground-up whole tea leaves, matcha has 137 times more antioxidants than regularly brewed green tea and a high level of easily absorbable dietary fiber. It also has a high content of L-theanine, an amino acid that helps balance the caffeine in the tea. Matcha has an earthy, somewhat grassy taste, but for me, its much deeper taste than regular green tea is better. It's definitely worth a try. I love it. In Japan, it's made using a bamboo bowl, sticks, and bamboo whisk. You can see how to do it on YouTube and enjoy it the Japanese way. In my busy life, I don't bother with that, but I do use a ceramic bowl and plastic whisk. I take time to sip it and breathe in between sips and make it into a small tea meditation. It helps a lot during a stressful day, but it does have a high caffeine content, so be sure to drink it at least six hours before you go to sleep.

The benefits of fresh-grown herbs:

Most herbs are weeds, which is the source of their potency. They can survive in all kinds of soil and air temperatures and can spread rapidly, taking over your garden if you're not careful. Peppermint is one of the aggressive types and best grown in a container. Most culinary and medicinal herbs are easily grown and carefree, and will come back every spring. (Some culinary herbs are also medicinal, like sage, which is anti-inflammatory, or peppermint, used for gastric problems.) This excludes basil, which has a low germination rate and requires warm temperatures and care.

I always encourage my patients to grow their own herbs for culinary purposes. Seasoning with fresh herbs is easy and makes your food much tastier and healthier. You don't need to make heavy sauces; just add fresh herbs to your dish while cooking. If you don't have a yard, then grow herbs in small containers on the windowsill. You only need to add sun and water. As I mentioned, they're very potent, and you don't need a lot to make your favorite dish taste great. I use them all the time in my kitchen, and also put herbs in my smoothies.

Garden sage

Flowering peppermint. Can you spot a bee there?

Basil is easy to grow when established.

Italian parsley

Baby cilantro and baby dill

Flowering tarragon

Chapter 18 | 71

Flowering rosemary bush

Thyme is very easy to grow. It will grow everywhere and spreads easily.

Oregano

Some, like rosemary, thyme, and parsley, grow all year long in the southern U.S. I use sage in chicken and fish dishes, thyme and parsley in almost every dish, marjoram in pork and beef, and rosemary for chicken, fish, and lamb. Rosemary is also delicious when used for roasted or cut and baked potatoes with yellow squash and some butter. Just cut fresh rosemary in very small pieces and sprinkle it over your dish before baking or roasting.

One of my favorite herbs is cilantro, which comes from the leaves and stems of the coriander plant, related to cumin, dill, fennel, and anise. Easy to grow, it reseeds itself in the late fall and grows during the entire winter and into spring in the southern part of the country. I can pick fresh and fragrant leaves even in winter. However, it dies out during the hot summer days. It's great in salads and soups and chicken and fish dishes.

Some research suggests that cilantro may accelerate the removal of heavy metals from our bodies. New research also indicates that it has a significant calming effect, and I agree. Just try to smell the fresh leaves and breathe for a while. Therefore, it may be a good candidate for a natural treatment for anxiety. High doses of cilantro extract have been found to have a similar effect to Valium, the medicine used for anxiety, but without its side effects and addictive qualities (Mahendra, P. and Bisht, S. 2011). It also has some antibacterial properties and may lower blood sugar. When your cilantro plants go to seed in the summer, don't discard the seeds. These little round seeds in semicircular clusters are coriander seeds. They're ornamental in addition to being tasty. Harvest the stems with the seeds and put them into your dry flower arrangements for the winter. Then pinch some seeds from the stems when you cook and add them to your favorite soups or meat dishes to enhance the flavor. Such a versatile plant! Try it.

There are many more herbs, such as tarragon, laurel leaves, chives, even lavender, that can be used in your favorite dishes. Have fun experimenting with them. Try seasoning with herbs, possibly fresh ones from your garden, from your herb pot in the kitchen, or from the store, instead of with heavy sauces that usually have a lot of calories and unhealthy additives. Fresh herbs will add an amazing flavor to your homemade meals and will help you stay slim and healthy. Bon appétit!

Eat your dandelions:

Dandelions, those annoying weeds in the middle of your beautiful lawn, are a huge and amazing antioxidant powerhouse. Their anti-inflammatory health benefit properties have been known for centuries. They may help cleanse the liver and kidneys, and also contain vitamin C, B_6, thiamin, riboflavin, calcium, iron, potassium, magnesium, folate, phosphorus, zinc, and copper. They are used in a variety of dishes, especially in Italian cuisine. You can make delicious dandelion soup, but you'll get the most benefit by using them in salads. If you don't like the taste, since it can be bitter, put dandelions into a smoothie with other greens and fruits, and you won't even notice the taste. Please remember that *the bitterer they are, the better they are for you*, since the bitterest ones have the most antioxidant power and health benefits.

Dandelions grow everywhere, so they're easy to find. However, don't use the ones from your lawn if you're using pesticides or a nonorganic fertilizer. Also, don't pick them from high traffic or pollution areas or from the part of your yard that's close to the areas that can be contaminated by your four-legged friends. The best place to pick them is from an area

Flowering dandelions

that's reasonably pollution-free or to let them grow in one part of your garden or yard. You can use the whole plant in smoothies or use the leaves in a salad. You can also buy dandelion leaves in health food stores, but the wild-grown ones usually have more antioxidant potency, especially in early spring before they start flowering. Just pick the whole green rosette of young leaves with the root, clean the root and leaves, and put the whole plant into your smoothie.

One more important thing: If you have allergies to plants or weeds or you're taking medications, please talk to your doctor before eating dandelions, since they may cause some allergies and interact with certain medications. The same applies to the plants mentioned in the next paragraphs.

Eat wild purslane:

Not everybody knows that purslane, an annoying weed that pops out in abundance in fields, gardens, walls, and sidewalk cracks, is packed with nutrients. Michael Pollan, author of *The Omnivore's Dilemma* (2006), calls it one of the two "most nutritious plants in the world." Purslane is a perennial succulent that grows close to the ground. It has paddle-shaped green leaves, pink or red stems, and tiny yellow flowers. The leaves, tender stems, and flowers can be eaten. Purslane has a slightly sour and salty, piquant taste. Its seeds are used in herbal drinks.

Wild purslane

Purslane was used in the ancient world as a medicinal herb and is still used for some inflammatory and other medical conditions. Because it's packed with omega-3 fatty acids, it also reduces the risk of heart disease. Purslane is cultivated for culinary purposes and used in African, Middle Eastern, and Mexican cuisine. It's low in fat and calories but rich in dietary fiber, vitamins, and minerals. It contains more omega-3 essential fatty acids (alpha-linolenic acid) than any other leafy plant. Therefore, it can be a good source of omega-3 fatty acid for vegans who prefer not to eat fish.

Purslane is high in vitamin A, C, E, B-complex, iron, magnesium, calcium, beta-carotene, and more (Uddin, K. et al. 2014). It contains two types of betalain alkaloid pigments that are powerful antioxidants and have been found to have antimutagenic properties in laboratory studies (Caballero-Salazar, S. et al. 2002). However, it also contains oxalic acid. For sensitive people, diets high in oxalic acid (also present in spinach, rhubarb, and peanuts) have been linked to an increased risk of kidney stones. If you have a family history of kidney stones or have the condition yourself, you may need to avoid eating plants high in oxalic acid. For the rest of us, purslane can be used in smoothies, soups, salads, stir-fries, etc. It can also be added to fish, pork, eggs, or whatever you like. You can even make a purslane pesto.

If you don't like the taste of purslane but still want to use it for its many health benefits, then put it in your smoothie. You won't taste it much or may not taste it at all when mixed with many other ingredients. Unlike the leaves of wild dandelions, which wilt fast, purslane can be kept in a fridge for three to four days. You can also dry purslane for winter use if you wish. I hope I've made you want to try this versatile plant, which is easy to get since it's actually a common weed.

Try edible flowers:

Edible flowers taste great and look beautiful on your plate, especially on top of your favorite salad. There are many edible flowers, but *not all* flowers are edible. You can find the complete list of edible flowers with pictures on the internet. Please use flowers from your garden only if you grow them organically

Calendula

Flowers of yellow squash with "visiting" bee inside one of them

without exposure to pesticides or artificial fertilizers, or grow them in pots away from pollution. You can use flowers like nasturtiums or some begonias or flowers of culinary herbs, such as violet flowers of sage, and some medicinal herbs such as beautiful and fragrant blue flowers of rosemary. The flowers usually taste similar to the leaves, but some may be spicier, like rosemary flowers. Also, don't use them in large quantities, since they may cause digestive problems. Use them sparingly in your dishes for great taste or as a garnish. Less is better.

In my kitchen, I love to use nasturtiums, which taste great and have antimicrobial and some anti-inflammatory properties. They're easy to grow and can reseed themselves, but since

Nasturtium

they're frost sensitive, you can only enjoy them outside until the first frost. The flowers and leaves have a somewhat spicy flavor. They taste great in salads and look beautiful on top. I also put them in soups and smoothies with other flowers like lavender, squash blossoms, arugula flowers, borage flowers, and petals of calendula. I use calendula petals in rice and grain dishes as well, since it is a medicinal herb with strong anti-inflammatory properties. Also, chamomile flowers have been known for centuries to have anti-inflammatory and anti-anxiety properties. However, the taste is quite bitter, so avoid this by using them in your smoothies so you still get the health benefits. Try some of the edible flowers in your kitchen and have fun with them.

The "Thursday soup"—quick and tasty French sorrel soup:

French sorrel soup—I call it the "Thursday soup," since I cook it once in a while on Thursdays when I feel tired, have nothing else to eat, having finished my leftovers on Wednesday, and don't feel like doing a lot of cooking or going out to eat. It's quick, and if you like the sharp taste of sorrel, it's just enough to fill you up without putting on too many calories. Sorrel is a perennial herb and has almost no fat. I cook it from the fresh leaves of French sorrel from my garden. French sorrel is a member of the buckwheat family and native to Europe. It has large, spinach-like leaves, and grows very well without any care once you buy a starter plant from the nursery.

French sorrel coming back in the spring

French sorrel has a milder taste than common sorrel, which grows wild in pastures and woods. Different varieties of sorrel have various amounts of oxalic acid. As I mentioned before, diets high in oxalic acid have been linked to an increased risk of kidney stones, so if you have a problem with this or a family history of kidney stones, talk to your doctor about your diet. For the rest of us, it's good to have a sorrel soup once in a while or to have oxalic acid from other plant sources. Oxalic acid is important for colon health, and if there isn't enough of it in our diet, the body makes it from ascorbic acid. If you have concerns about the amount of oxalic acid in sorrel, buy your starter plants in a nursery where they're bred to be low oxalic and you may have your favorite soup more frequently. Below is how I do it— quick and easy. You can use sorrel from your garden or buy fresh sorrel leaves in any health food store.

Start by cutting half an onion or a small onion into little pieces, depending on how much you like in your dish. Simmer the onion in a deep skillet or shallow pot with olive oil for several minutes until the onion turns clear. You can add some minced garlic if you like. In the meantime, pick your sorrel leaves, preferably young and tender, from the garden, or use a sorrel bunch that you picked up from the store—let's say on your way home. You may need about half a pound per person. Wash and drain the sorrel in a salad spinner and cut into medium pieces. Add about a tablespoon of butter to the skillet, add the sorrel, and sauté for around ten minutes.

In the meantime, hard-boil one or two eggs in a different pot. After you've sautéed the sorrel (it will turn dark green), you can add some vegetable broth, chicken broth, or water to the desired consistency and boil it. Add salt and pepper to your taste, and it's ready. You can also add sour cream or coconut cream if you like.

Remove the shells from the hard-boiled eggs, cut them in half, and place them in a bowl. Pour your soup into the bowl, and here is your quick and easy dinner. You can also use leftover potatoes instead of eggs. It tastes good either way. Enjoy!

Don't forget about the red wine:

Research shows that there's a health benefit from red wine if drunk in moderation: one glass per day for women and two for men. Red wine contains many antioxidants, especially resveratrol, which are good for your health. Resveratrol protects against heart disease and cancer. It is found in the skin of the grapes, and the type of grape with the most is my favorite, a purple grape that produces Pinot Noir. Enjoy.

The Mediterranean diet:

Many nutrition experts agree that the healthiest way to eat is to follow the Mediterranean diet because of its polyphenols, plant-based compounds found in these foods (Zamora-Ros et al. 2013). Much research shows a lot of health benefits in this diet (Grosso, G. et al. 2017; Rosato, V. et al. 2017; Petersson, S. D. and Philippou, E. 2016; Pounis, G. et al. 2018). It's the "heart friendly" diet that lowers the risk of cardiovascular disease as well as "bad" cholesterol. New research has shown that people eating this diet have a 60 percent reduction in cardiovascular risk (Bonaccio, M. et al. 2017). Since the Mediterranean diet is plant-based, it provides a lot of fiber needed for a well-functioning digestive tract.

This diet includes fruits, vegetables, lots of greens, fish and seafood, whole grains, legumes, nuts, healthy fats like olive oil and avocado, fresh herbs and spices, and, of course, red wine.

Chicken cacciatore, an easy-to-make and popular Italian dish. You can find many recipes on the internet. Read some of them and try your own.

The other important part of the Mediterranean diet is its social aspect. People from the Mediterranean region like to eat their meals with family and friends. We need to remember that eating is not only for nutrition but is also a social event stemming from ancient times when people were hunting, fishing, and eating together. Research shows that when we eat with family and friends and have conversation during meals, we eat less and take more time to chew the food, which is a very healthy way to eat.

The calorie restriction diet:
A growing set of literature suggests that longevity and good health are related to the calorie restriction diet (Fung, J. 2016; Longo, V. D. and Mattson, M. P. 2014). Simply put, it indicates that we need to eat less overall or fast one or two days a week. If you're a full-time working person, it may be difficult to fast a whole day, but you can probably eat less than normal one or two days per week and still get some benefit. Also, some health care professionals believe that intermittent fasting has great health benefits. Intermittent fasting means that you have your last meal at 7 p.m. and don't eat anything until 7 a.m. or 11 a.m. the next day. Working people may have a problem with that on weekdays, but it can be done more easily on weekends,

when most people tend to sleep longer. As with everything in life, try to do your best, and don't get anxious if a regular fasting routine is not your thing. If you try to eat healthy and do fast once in a while, it will still have some health benefits.

However, if you have a medical condition such as diabetes, a calorie restriction diet may not be the best option. In *The Obesity Code* (2016), which Dr. Jason Fung based on his experience treating patients with Type 2 diabetes, he argues that cutting calories is not a good idea because most people have difficulty tolerating feeling hungry. He recommends instead a low-carb, high-fat diet which makes people feel satiated and results in lower insulin levels. Always talk to your physician before trying any kind of diet.

If you want to live longer and be healthy up to the end of your life, it may be a good idea to research and practice the calorie restriction diet.

Drink your meals:

Make a delicious smoothie from whatever greens, fruits, and vegetables you have in the fridge or in your garden, and drink your lunch or dinner instead of cooking it. It'll fill you up and can make you slimmer because it usually has fewer calories than a regular meal and is much easier to digest.

Patients frequently ask me about recipes for smoothies. It's easy to make them, and you really don't need a recipe. Put into a blender whatever you like and have at home (e.g., fresh or frozen berries, fruits, leafy greens like spinach, kale, and arugula, some veggies, and some nuts). Pour almond milk, yogurt, or kefir (which has the most probiotics) into the blender, blend, and enjoy. You can experiment with different ingredients and have fun doing it.

I always try to have berries in my smoothies, especially blueberries. Sometimes they're called "God's candies" because they improve blood flow to the brain, increase brain activity, and improve memory (Bowtell, J. L. et al. 2017; Kirkorian, R. et al. 2010; Papandreou, M. A. et al. 2009). Berries can be expensive because they spoil fast if not sold and eaten quickly. Sometimes they look good in the package, but when you open it at home, half the package is spoiled. Therefore, most of the time, I use organic frozen blueberries, although sometimes raspberries and cranberries, which are also antioxidant powerhouses. (Cranberries also help your urinary tract stay healthy.) Frozen berries are already washed and frozen fresh, so they keep most of their nutritional value, and, what is very important, are less expensive.

You can add strawberries to your smoothie if you like. They're less expensive, and available fresh most of the year. I also always add a small piece of fresh turmeric root because of its antioxidant and anti-inflammatory properties, and about an inch of fresh ginger root because of its anti-inflammatory, antibacterial, and antiviral properties. During the cold and flu season, I also put pumpkin seeds in my smoothie because they contain zinc, which helps fight infections. Since I'm in private practice, I don't have paid sick leave. When I'm sick, I have no income but still have bills to pay, which makes preventing colds and flu a priority.

Healthy breakfast: To eat or not to eat?

I'm paraphrasing Hamlet's famous question because it's important, although there's no consensus as to whether you should or should not eat breakfast. Some research shows that it *is* important to do this within two hours of waking to speed up your metabolism. But other studies indicate that skipping breakfast has no significant negative effect on your health and may help you lose weight.

I believe you should do whatever your body tells you. It may be perfectly normal for you to skip breakfast if you don't feel hungry in the morning and can wait until lunchtime to have your first meal. *Don't* forget, though, to drink water, juice, tea, coffee, etc. in the morning to stay hydrated, and then have a healthy brunch or lunch when you feel hungry. *Don't* snack the whole day and eat a large meal in the evening. This will only cause you to gain weight. If you need to have breakfast, try to make it a healthy one. This means what your body needs. For some people, it will be a big meal with eggs, sausages, and potatoes. For others, it may be a small or moderate one.

For those who need to eat something small and healthy in the morning, I suggest overnight oatmeal, the perfect breakfast for busy people. I do it myself. It has both a health benefit and a timesaving benefit in the morning because you prepare it the evening before and keep it in the fridge. Oatmeal has been eaten for generations because of its incredibly nutritious and satiation benefits. It contains powerful soluble fiber and many vitamins and minerals, such as magnesium, copper, iron, vitamin B, etc. that help lower blood sugar and prevent heart disease. It's a carbohydrate that you can eat in the morning if you're trying to reduce daily carbohydrate intake.

I use a simple recipe, but you can find a lot of variations on the internet. I put three tablespoons of organic, old-fashioned rolled oats in a mug and add one-half to one tablespoon of chia seeds (mainly for omega-3 fatty acids benefits) and hemp seeds (for hormonal balance and improved digestion). I don't have time to measure exactly, and I also don't think it matters. Then I add a few shakes of ground cinnamon (for lowering blood

Overnight oats with berries (author's breakfast) are easy to make, healthy, and tasty. Recipe in this chapter.

sugar) and a shake or two of ground turmeric and ground ginger (for their powerful anti-inflammatory benefits). I add some yogurt or kefir, stir, and add almond milk to make it a creamy soup consistency. I stir a few more times and put it in the fridge. In the morning, I have a creamy and delicious oatmeal that I top with fresh (if available) but usually frozen berries. It's a real morning treat. Try it.

I also put ground cinnamon, turmeric, and ginger in my coffee for their anti-inflammatory benefits. The best way is to shake some of them into the basket of your coffee maker to blend in before brewing. This kind of morning coffee will really wake you up and make you feel great the rest of your day.

I need to mention here the research on curcumin, which is a main ingredient in turmeric, the one that gives it its intense yellow color. In addition to its anti-inflammatory benefits, curcumin can reduce anxiety and depression and induce brain plasticity. In India, where it is used commonly, there are much lower rates of cancer and Alzheimer's disease than in the U.S. and other Western countries. I like turmeric, so I sprinkle it on all meats and fish before cooking and put it in my soups. It really makes meals much tastier and more colorful.

The benefit of slow cooking:

If you don't have a slow cooker or Crock-Pot, I hope you'll get one. It makes delicious, healthy meals and is a real timesaver for a busy person. Usually, you can put in all your ingredients in the morning and have a delightful dinner in the evening, although sometimes you add some tender vegetables the last hour of the cooking. Slow cooking improves the flavor and texture of your meals and gives you more health benefits. First of all, you're in charge of what you put in the Crock-Pot and can modify recipes to your liking by adding more vegetables or herbs. Food cooked at lower heat for several hours usually has more nutrient content than food that is boiled or fried. Also, when you use the juices from your slow-cooking food, you're adding back the nutrients that were released while the food was being cooked. Meals cooked in a Crock-Pot may also have fewer calories and less fat, so why not try it?

There are many good recipes on the internet. One important healthy soup that's best made in a Crock-Pot is bone soup. This is truly nourishing to your body, especially in the winter or if you feel sluggish, ill, or want to get stronger after experiencing health problems. Bone soup has been used as folk medicine for generations. It has great nutritional benefits and can best be cooked in a Crock-Pot on the slow function for many hours. You can also cook it on the stove, as was done for generations, but you have to pay attention to it. You can find many bone soup recipes on the internet. Make sure the main ingredients you use (bones) come from animals that were organically fed and/or pasture raised. If you're truly interested in healthy eating, try some recipes for bone soup and other delicious meals. You'll love cooking with a Crock-Pot.

~19~
The Importance of a Good Night's Sleep

A GROWING AMOUNT OF RESEARCH INDICATES THAT A good night's sleep is very important not only for our physical health and ability to function but mainly for our brain's health as a preventive factor against Alzheimer's dementia. The number of hours researchers say we need varies from six to eight. Dr. R. Tanzi, a prominent brain researcher, believes most people need eight hours of sleep. He and other researchers suggest that while we sleep, our brain is getting "cleaned" of the harmful substances that accumulate there during our daily activities, which protects the brain from disease (Chopra, D. and Tanzi, R. E. 2015 and 2018).

A good night's sleep—no question—makes people feel better. According to Dan Buettner, a journalist who researched the "Blue Zones" (areas of the world where people live long and healthy lives), those who sleep less than six hours report feeling 30 percent less happy than others who sleep seven and a half to nine hours (Buettner, D. 2008). The quality of sleep is also important. Most busy people tend to cut down on sleep to complete their tasks, but this is not a good idea. If you want a well-functioning brain, you need to get a good night's sleep.

In my practice, I've noticed that many patients have difficulty sleeping, and most of them take sleeping pills. However, before you reach for a pill, it's important to find out why you're unable to sleep and try to deal with the problem that's causing it, be it pain, anxiety, stress, racing thoughts, etc. A pill is a quick and easy solution, but it comes with a hefty price. According to new research, long-term use of sleeping pills suppresses brain activity, which may lead to dementia (Chen, PL et al. 2012; Billioti de Gage, S. et al. 2012; Shih, H. et al. 2015).

If you have difficulty sleeping and don't want to take sleep medications, there are other things you can do. Try herbal teas designed to relax you, like chamomile tea, valerian root, or a mixture of herbs that are in the teas designed for a good night's sleep. You can easily find them in health food stores. If the ready-made tea doesn't work, talk to an oriental medicine doctor, herbalist, or naturopathic doctor who will design a tea especially for you.

If drinking tea before you go to bed doesn't help, try the Buddhist's tea meditation that I describe in detail in Chapter 26. It's very relaxing. I do it myself to calm down after a stressful day, and it works well. I also teach my patients to do it, telling them not to give up easily but to continue for a while. Some of them like it and say that it helps. You can also try your favorite meditation or any kind of relaxation that works for you, such as a lavender aromatic bath.

The general rule is that if you cannot fall asleep, instead of tossing and turning, get up from the bed and start doing something mundane, like reading a boring paper. Don't work on your computer or check your smartphone because the blue light they emit stimulates the brain. If pain keeps you awake, try physical therapy instead of pain meds which can interfere with your sleep. If stress and/or anxiety keeps you awake, try meditation (Nagendra, R.P. et al. 2012). In a case of chronic insomnia, I recommend seeing a sleep specialist and sleep studies to rule out apnea or a sleep breathing disorder.

~20~
The Power of Physical Exercise

Life is like riding a bicycle: To keep your balance, you must keep moving.
—Albert Einstein

According to an old saying, "If you don't use it, you lose it." That applies to everything in life, especially physical and mental activity. I'll cover mental exercises later, but let me talk about physical exercises first. A huge amount of research links physical activity to brain health (Macpherson, H. et al. 2017; Benedict, C. et al. 2013; Erickson, K. I. et al. 2010). Some research suggests that exercising is the best Alzheimer's prevention (Panza, G. A. et al. 2018; Erickson, K. I. and Kramer, A. F. 2009; Hess, N. C. L. et.al 2014). In one of the most important studies, published in the *Proceedings of the National Academy of Sciences* (Erickson, K. I. et al. 2011), the results indicated that adults who walked forty minutes three times a week for one year had brain growth in the hippocampus, the area of the brain most important for memory functioning.

When we exercise, our brain releases more serotonin and endorphins, which are "feel good" hormones, and also increases the flow of oxygen-rich blood to the brain. Generally, simple exercises like walking and jogging can be a very good antidote for stress, sadness, depression, anxiety, etc. When you have a bad day and feel like life has too many strains, instead of submerging yourself in depressive or anxiety-generating thoughts, grab a jacket and walking shoes and go outside. Walk or jog and see the beauty of nature that is everywhere around you, even in the middle of town on a rainy day. Look at the clouds. If you don't have enough strength that day, just sit outside and breathe.

Please remember that anxiety and depression do not facilitate healing, so get some exercise. Most research suggests that you need only thirty minutes of brisk walking five times a week to get the benefit of good health. However, any kind of physical activity counts, and even a little bit a day is better than nothing.

My patients always ask me what the best exercise regimen would be. I agree with Dr. Christiane Northrup: the one you're doing. The important thing about exercising is that you do it with *joy*. If you start an exercise that you were told would be best but don't like it, you'll stop after a while, so find something you do enjoy and try it a few times a week. The best practice is some kind of physical activity every day, but if you're too busy, do it a few times a week.

As I mentioned, every kind of physical activity counts, especially on a regular basis. Don't try to do too much. Start with one kind of activity, e.g., daily walking. If you have a dog, let your dog take you for a walk. You and your four-legged friend will love it. If you do a mindful walk (details on this in the next chapter), you'll get both physical and a spiritual benefit. You'll feel connected to Mother Nature.

When you have succeeded in being persistent with daily walking, you can add other physical activity such as strength training. You don't need an expensive gym membership. Most strength and resistance exercises can be done using your own body weight or small, inexpensive dumbbells and/or resistance bands, which you can buy in the nearest sporting goods store. However, if you like to see other people exercising around you, especially if it motivates you, then the gym is a good place. If you're a senior citizen, you can get a discount at most gyms. Also, you may be able to get a free or discounted membership through your health insurance company. They are big on preventing health problems nowadays because healthy members cost them much less than sick ones do.

If you cannot motivate yourself to exercise regularly, or you think you don't have enough time, hire a personal trainer and set up regular appointments. The trainer will be waiting for you at the gym or at home, so you'll have to exercise no matter how tired or unmotivated you feel. If you start doing it regularly, it may become a good habit which you'll miss if you can't do it, such as when you're traveling.

Just a note: I wrote this chapter after thirty minutes of walking and jogging. I feel much better after exercising. Before my walking and jogging, I felt like my writing was getting slower and wasn't that creative. I'm in my 60s and started jogging only several months ago. I don't have the endurance to jog for the whole thirty minutes yet, but that's my goal. Therefore, I do a modified interval training in which I alternate periods of high-intensity exercise with low-intensity exercise. According to physical training authorities, it's the best way to get fit. I walk for a while and then I jog for a while.

I don't carry a stopwatch, but to measure my progress, I jog from one speed bump on the road to another and then walk to the next one and then jog again. I've been doing this for a while, and now I can jog the whole distance between speed bumps, which I couldn't do before. I don't know if this is the best way to measure progress, but it's working for me. I encourage you to do the same. If you don't have speed bumps, find other markers on your walking/jogging route (e.g., trees, stop signs, mile markers, etc.).

I have to mention one important safety rule. If you're a woman and exercising alone, for your own safety, do *not* use headphones when walking or jogging outside. You need to be aware of your surroundings. Also, do *not* walk the same trail all the time. Change your route daily if possible, but go to the trail with your own "marks" once in a while to measure your progress in jogging.

The best way to exercise and not lose your motivation is to get a friend or a group of friends to exercise with you. You'll be motivating each other. Being with friends makes the time much nicer and seem to go faster, which makes a difference, especially if you want to do longer distances.

~21~
The Importance of Practicing Yoga

I RECOMMEND PRACTICING YOGA TO MOST OF MY PATIENTS if there are no medical contraindications. I do it myself. I'm not a yoga master, just a strong believer in its therapeutic ability. I believe it helps you center the body, mind, and spirit, and to manage stress (Woodyard, C. 2011; Krishnakumar, D. et al. 2015). If you're a beginner, it's best to go to yoga classes, which you can easily find in your neighborhood or on TV or the internet, or you can buy a yoga CD.

Yoga helps you focus on the present moment and increases your body's flexibility and ability to tolerate pain and discomfort. I can swear to it. I have chronic pain due to scoliosis, yet don't take any pain pills because I start my day with yoga stretches and other exercises, sun or rain.

Yoga also helps you shift your mental state from a negative to a positive focus. It has many other medical benefits as well, such as improving respiration and maintaining a balanced metabolism, and mental health benefits like reducing anxiety and improving concentration. New research suggests that practicing yoga may be important for people who have been exposed to trauma. Regular talk therapy may not be enough to treat trauma because the experiences that cause it live in structures of the brain that don't respond to words. Therefore, body-based practices like yoga have a positive impact on the health and well-being of trauma survivors (Jindani, F. et al. 2015; Cramer, H. et al. 2018).

~22~
The Power of Active Learning and Positive Brain Stimulation

LEARNING IS POWERFUL. INDIA'S LEADER AND PEACE ACTIvist Mahatma Gandhi (1869–1948) once said, "Learn like you are going to live forever and live like you are going to die tomorrow."

One of the best exercises for your brain is active learning. It can be something related to your hobby or passion or simply doing something you've never done before but always wanted to do. This can be learning a foreign language, playing an instrument, starting piano lessons, learning how to dance or paint, or planning a trip to a foreign country. Planning travel and travel itself are great learning experiences, especially if you need to learn a new country's language to communicate with the people there. Planning a trip requires you to study the region you're going to. Then you'll have to prepare a schedule for your trip. When it's under way, not everything will go according to plans. You'll have to react to new and unforeseen situations that will definitely happen while you're traveling.

Many years ago, it was believed that the brain makes new connections only for the first several years of our life. Now the research says something different: that the brain makes new connections between neurons until the end of our life, especially if we stay cognitively active. So instead of sitting and thinking about what will happen to your brain when you get older, considering that there's so much scary news about dementia, start thinking on the positive side and change your thoughts. Ask yourself, "What exciting and interesting new things can I learn?" and then start doing it.

The title of this chapter talks about "positive" brain stimulation. This means learning something that brings you some joy, or at least peace. You need to find an activity that makes you feel good, not just something your friends or family members are doing, or something you were told was good for you. Even if you've invested money in a particular learning project, it won't work for you in the long run if you don't really like doing it. Soon you'll start avoiding it. Nevertheless, try to be open to new learning experiences, even if at the beginning, they don't sound like a very good idea. You could start learning something because your spouse wanted you to, even though you've never actually liked it (e.g., ballroom dancing), and then find it quite rewarding. By staying open-minded, you may find unexpected things that make you feel good about learning them and will also boost your self-esteem.

Active, lifelong learning is important for people who suffer from any kind of brain trauma because, as I've said, if you don't use it, you lose it. Sometimes they have to relearn things like walking, talking, and taking care of themselves. However, after they master basic abilities, it's important to keep the brain stimulated by learning new things, especially if they bring joy and satisfaction.

I always encourage my patients to return to school if their cognitive abilities have remained relatively good, or to learn a new trade if they can no longer do a previous job. We give them a letter of accommodation which most schools accept and then follow our recommendations. I also advise my patients to start learning something new just for fun. It may turn into a part-time job (if that's as much as they can work). There's no reason to give up on yourself and your dreams just because you've had a brain problem. You are more than your brain problems.

I'd like to include here a famous quote from a person who overcame the virtually impossible, American author and activist Helen Keller (1880–1968). The first deaf and blind person to earn a bachelor of arts degree, she once said:

> *Keep your face to the sunshine and you cannot see the shadows. It's what the sunflowers do.*

You can try "brain games":
A variety of "brain games" are available on the internet which you can also play on your smartphone. Most of them are designed for the aging population to stimulate different parts of the brain and improve different areas of functioning. For example, some work to improve verbal comprehension and others to improve reasoning on visual material. Some are free and others are expensive.

The research results related to brain games may be confusing. Some suggests that they help improve brain functions while other research has found there isn't much benefit (Stanmore, E. et al. 2017; Zelinski, E. M. and Reyes, R. 2009; Edwards, J. D. et al. 2017). Of course, it depends on the game itself. Some are more challenging and stimulating than others. As a neuropsychologist with more than thirty years of experience, I believe the benefit depends on what your brain problems are and what game or set of games you're using. I also strongly believe that any kind of brain exercise is better than none. Aging brains, just like aging muscles, need their daily dose of exercise.

If you're an aging person who sits around and complains about getting older, you'll definitely age faster than a someone who is mentally and physically active. Start with websites that are free. For example, if you're over fifty and a member of AARP, you can log on to its website and play brain games free. You can also do crosswords and other puzzles in your daily newspaper or in a magazine or can subscribe to puzzle magazines, which aren't that expensive.

You can also play logic puzzles, "smart games," I.Q. puzzle games, "construction games," brain teasers, or puzzles made from bamboo, such as "star puzzles" that you need to deconstruct first and then reassemble. Working with plastic, wood, or metal puzzles engages your tactile sensory pathways in addition to visual and visual-motor abilities. The more senses you can engage in a task, the more exercise your brain will be getting simultaneously.

Try to do your brain games every day or every other day, especially if you're retired, stay home most of the time, and don't have much cognitively stimulating activity. If you're still working full-time or part-time doing something cognitively challenging, like advanced computer programming, creative writing, managing, etc., you're exercising your brain enough. However, you can still do crossword puzzles or play brain games for fun. The *New England Journal of Medicine* (Verghese, J. et al. 2003) reported the results of a study indicating that elderly people who did crossword puzzles four times a week had a 47 percent lower risk of dementia than subjects who did puzzles once a week. *Wow!*

Patients frequently ask me how much time they should spend daily or weekly playing brain games. It depends on many factors. The main one is your access to the internet. If you don't have access at home, you can go to the nearest public library or to a senior citizens center. The other important factor is your ability to concentrate and to work on the computer or your smartphone without experiencing physical pain, which often is associated with aging.

If you're getting tired or making more mistakes than usual or having pain, you need to stop and rest or stretch. If the break isn't enough, stop for that day and start fresh the next one. Hopefully, you'll be able to do the work a little longer the next day.

The time that you spend on cognitive stimulation is better than sitting and complaining about your life circumstances, including getting older. Please remember that depression and anxiety do not facilitate cognitive progress and healing. Generally speaking, I believe an hour a day (or thirty minutes twice a day) of brain games should be enough. If you like doing more, then keep on. Don't forget about taking breaks, eating regularly, and especially going for your daily walk and doing your daily physical exercises. These are also good ways to stimulate your brain.

Also, try to play word games or any other cognitively stimulating games with your family and turn it into a family event. Don't forget to make it joyful and fun, even if you're having some problems at the beginning. It'll get better with practice.

If you think you may have problems in brain functioning and are not sure which games would be most beneficial, you should start by being evaluated by a neuropsychologist. Afterward, the neuropsychologist will be able to tell you what kind of problems you have and what kind of brain games may help the most. Also, if you or a family member suffered a TBI or other neurological problem and wants to start doing brain games or any other cognitive stimulation, it will be better to first complete a neuropsychological evaluation. Then discuss with the neuropsychologist which kind of brain exercises will be most beneficial.

You can try neurofeedback:
Neurofeedback is a computer-guided, noninvasive brain-function training based on EEG feedback. It is also called "neurotherapy," "neurobiofeedback," or "electroencephalography (EEG) biofeedback," which helps control involuntary processes such as muscle tension and heart rate. Usually, the subject is responding to a computer display of her or his own brain's electrical activity, but it may also simply be sound stimulation. The most important factor is that neurofeedback is focusing on helping a person *train himself or herself* to regulate brain functions. The technique is used to help treat a variety of neurological and mental health conditions such as concussions, stroke, migraines, anxiety, depression, sleep problems, chronic pain, and PTSD. A review of the literature suggests that it's most promising so far in helping treat ADHD in children by enhancing self-regulation, which improves attention and reduces impulsivity (Cortese, S. et al. 2016). It also helps enhance mental sharpness in adults (Staufenbiel, S. M. et al. 2014).

For a variety of neurological and mental health conditions, research results are inconclusive, but some people who have tried it believe that it works. It is not a treatment program but helps to facilitate healing in a person who attends therapy and tries to live a healthy lifestyle. It may also help the person get better with fewer medications or hopefully without meds at all in the long run. However, it isn't covered by most insurance plans, usually costs $100 per session, and may require ten or more sessions, so the financial burden might be significant. If you can afford it, it's worth a try, since any positive and goal-oriented brain stimulation exercises are good for you. You can easily find neurofeedback providers in your area on the internet.

Daily reading:

Reading stimulates your brain, decreases your stress level, increases your vocabulary and knowledge, and improves your memory and concentration. It may also contribute to your longevity. A study published in *Social Science and Medicine* (Bavishi, A. et al. 2016) indicated that readers of at least a book chapter a day experienced a 20 percent reduction in risk of mortality over the twelve years of follow-up compared with non-book readers. Also, the study found, "book reading contributed to a survival advantage that was significantly greater than that observed for reading newspapers or magazines." Other studies suggest that reading any material about thirty minutes a day may be beneficial.

Generally, research suggests that reading, board games, playing a musical instrument, and dancing are associated with lower risk of dementia.

Listen to music:

The famous French novelist, poet, and dramatist Victor Hugo (1802-1885) once said, "Music expresses that which cannot be said and on which is impossible to be silent."

Over the past several years, many studies have suggested that certain kinds of music have a positive effect on our brain. For example, listening to Mozart may have positive effect on your cognitive functions (Verrusio, W. et al. 2015). Make sure to listen to music that will be uplifting, not something that makes you anxious or sad.

Go dancing:

Dancing is good for your body, mind, and spirit. It will cheer you up and may help you lose weight. Research on participants in tango lessons indicates that it may also improve memory, concentration, and brain plasticity (Israili, Z. H. and Israili, S. J. 2017). Besides, dancing is really good aerobic exercise and a lot of fun (Keogh, J. et al. 2009). If you think you're not the dancing type but still want to learn how, join a studio or club in your community. These are quite popular, and you should have no problem finding one. Most have reasonable prices because they're serving not only young people but also a growing population of healthy seniors. Dance instructors are very patient and will help you improve with practice. You only need to get there and enjoy.

If you're a single woman who likes to dance, you can try a belly dance class, since you don't need a partner. You can still get your exercise and have a lot of fun.

Use colors to brighten your day:

Colors can do more than you think. They can affect not only your mood but also your energy level, sleep pattern, blood pressure, and even sexuality (Elliot, A. J, 2015; Elliot, A. J. and Niesta, D. 2008). Some colors aren't good for us in the long run while others make us feel better and healthier, and will motivate us and improve concentration. Therefore, it's important to know how to use them. For example, the color white commonly used in most public spaces and schools can increase stress, decrease concentration, and be a catalyst for headaches.

Color is an important stimulus for our brain because 80 percent of our sensory impressions come from the visual system. Research suggests that the pituitary gland—which is responsible for body temperature, energy level, sleep pattern, metabolism, and sexuality—is sensitive to color stimulation (Gruson, L. 1982). Colors are light waves of different lengths, and they affect us even when we have our eyes closed. Therefore, we should pay attention to the colors in our homes and work spaces.

Warm colors such as yellow, orange, pink, and red can motivate and energize us. However, if they're too intense, they can also be irritating. Cool colors like green, blue, and violet can have a calming effect. Gray, which is commonly used in professional settings or formal events, can be more depressing than black. During the winter months, especially in the northern states, when everything looks white, gray, or black, it's good to wear bright colors because they can make us feel better. They can be our "emotional vitamins."

My favorite color is yellow, because I love sunshine and warm temperatures. In my office and my home, all walls are in shades of yellow to remind me, especially on dark and cold winter days, that spring and sunshine will come again. I also like pink because it's an uplifting color. Most of my tops are in shades of pink or fuchsia. Also, most of the beautiful wild or garden flowers are pink or fuchsia. When we wear shades of pink, we communicate to the outside world that we're sensitive and imaginative. Let's get creative with colors so we can brighten our outside and inside environments.

~23~
Gardening: Food for Body, Mind, and Spirit (and Very Good Brain Exercise)

As Audrey Hepburn beautifully said, "To plant a garden is to believe in tomorrow."

I totally agree. Not everybody knows that she was not only a brilliant actress but also an avid gardener. At her home in Switzerland, she had a big garden and used her crops for not only cooking but also making homemade preserves, juices, marmalades, etc.

I strongly believe that *food is our medicine*. Therefore, I encourage all my patients to garden wherever they can, even in pots on a balcony, patio, or the windowsill. Any form of gardening is good for your health. You're eating fresh produce full of great natural nutrients, not produce that's traveled long distances and been in groceries for who knows how long. Nowadays, there are many ways to preserve produce. When you grow your own vegetables, you can choose the seeds, and you know what fertilizers you put in. I encourage you to use organic seeds and fertilizers, and as a result, you'll know what you're eating.

Every day, you can make a fresh salad from varied combinations of greens and vegetables by picking a few leaves from different plants. *Yum!* This is so, so good. When you bring your garden treasures to the kitchen, you'll be overwhelmed by their fresh, natural, and wonderful smell. Your whole kitchen will smell like your garden. When I have friends over, I let them first smell the contents of my garden basket even before I prepare the salad, to let them experience the wonderful freshness of it.

Eating such a wonderful fresh meal is an experience for not only your body but also your mind and spirit. Eat slowly and taste the food's goodness. Its fresh smell will speak to your mind and make you feel better, not only physically but also

Author's garden in Albuquerque, New Mexico

emotionally. When you bring a feeling of pleasure to your mind, your spirit will brighten up.

As I mentioned previously, gardening is a great brain exercise. It requires a lot of planning and organizing, and you can see the results of your work. You'll need to make many decisions at the beginning of and throughout the growing season, since unexpected things may happen. You'll have to problem-solve all the time, which is great exercise for your brain.

You will have to decide what kinds of plants you want, how many, and where you'll place them in the garden. Try to grow some new things every year. You'll need to spend some time studying the new plants and deciding which would be best for your garden. You have to consider the climate (growing zone),

Fresh flowers in a vase will bring bright colors to your room and a beautiful natural fragrance.

your soil conditions, and how many hours of sun or shade the plants will need. Then, there's a planting time according to the schedule you've prepared. Most vegetables won't grow when the temperature is above 85 degrees Fahrenheit, so you'll have to plant them early in the season.

When it comes to solving problems in gardening, you'll learn a good deal from experience. Prepare for a lot of unexpected things. Some seeds may not germinate, even if you bought them from an expensive catalog, and you'll need to figure out what you can do next. You can look for other seeds or buy something different from a local nursery. When your plants are growing, they're subject to diseases, insects, and predators like gophers, pack rats, squirrels, and birds, which like to pick on the fresh and juicy sprouting seedlings. You'll have to observe carefully, learn to recognize problems, and know how to deal with them. When the plants mature, you can see their beauty and bring to the kitchen a full basket of fresh greens or veggies. This is your great reward, which is worth all that work.

Most people with a vegetable garden also have flowerbeds and perhaps a rose garden. They all require care, and working on them is also a very good brain exercise. Your work will be greatly rewarded when they're in bloom. You can bring flowers into the house, and they'll brighten the room and fill it with a beautiful fragrance. You can also meditate while looking at the beauty of the flowers and be thankful that you can see them, because the colors that you can see in nature cannot be compared with anything else.

~24~
Living in the Present: The Power of Mindfulness

Every breath we take, every step we make, can be filled with peace, joy, and serenity.
—Thich Nhat Hanh, author of *The Miracle of Mindfulness*

WHEN WE GO INTO THE PAST, WE CAN GO INTO DEPRESsion. When we go into the future, we can go into anxiety. The only thing we have is right now. Practicing living in the present is very important for your mental health and takes a heavy load of worry from your shoulders.

Even one of the oldest and most read books in the world, the Bible, tells us to live in the present and not worry about the future. Ecclesiastes 7:14 states: "When times are good, be happy; but when times are bad, consider this: God has made the one as well as the other. Therefore, no one can discover anything about the future." Also, Matthew 6:34 says: "Therefore do not worry about tomorrow, for tomorrow will worry about itself."

Isaiah 43:18 advises us to also not concentrate on the past: "Forget the former things; do not dwell on the past." Also, Ecclesiastes 7:10 tells us: "Do not say, 'Why were the old days better than these?' For it is not wise to ask such questions."

You can easily Google other Bible verses that tell you not to worry about the future or the past but to live in the present.

The practice of mindfulness, living in the present, originated in Tibet about 3,500 years ago, even before Buddha. It was popularized it in the U.S. and other Western countries by Jon Kabat-Zinn (1994, 2005, 2006). According to him, "Mindfulness is awareness that arises through paying attention, on purpose, in the present moment, nonjudgmentally." Generally speaking, mindfulness is the practice of present-moment awareness. It's about knowing what is on your mind.

I like the example of mindfulness that Kabat-Zinn frequently brings up in media interviews. He says something like this: If you're in the shower in the morning, just be in the shower, feeling the water coming down on your body, not in the meeting that you will have at work or other things you will have to do that day.

This frequently comes to me when I'm in the shower thinking about the upcoming day. I remind myself to just be in the shower. Practicing mindfulness is not easy at the beginning, but it gets much better with practice. Trust me and trust yourself.

Walks in nature are a good mindfulness practice:

I encourage all my patients to do mindful nature walks—to concentrate on walking and enjoying nature around you, breathing freely, and smelling Mother Nature. Even the grass and ordinary weeds on the side of the road can smell beautiful. Look up and see the color of the sky and the clouds. After your mindful walk, you should feel relaxed and energized at the same time.

~25~
Practice Gratitude for Mental Uplifting

Gratitude is the foundation of happiness. So if you want to start being happy, get grateful first.
—Oprah Winfrey

GRATITUDE IS THE PRACTICE OF FINDING GOOD IN EACH day. When you feel down or overstressed, it's best to shift your mental state and start thinking about all the blessings in your life, all the things that are working out for you. Making an effort to see the good in your life will almost immediately put you in a better mental state. You will simply feel better.

You can list your problems on the left side of the page and blessings on the right, and most of the time, the blessings list will be longer. It's difficult to get stuck on negatives when you're writing and counting your blessings. Research finds that people who practice gratitude daily have a better and healthier life. Practicing gratitude may help boost your immune system and lower blood pressure, and also help you cope better with stress, sleep better, and be less at risk of anxiety, depression, and substance abuse.

You don't need to medicate your depression, anxiety, or mood swings with substances, since you're medicating them with gratitude. Of course, in the case of severe mental problems, practicing gratitude won't be enough. You may need medications and intense therapy. However, practicing gratitude will definitely facilitate healing.

Try to savor your everyday life by slowing down and enjoying all the things that bring you peace and joy but that we take for granted: for example, that you are alive and generally healthy, and that there is sunshine in the morning and blue skies. Also, be grateful for your delicious cup of morning tea or coffee. Many people don't have this opportunity. I like to drink it looking at my garden in the morning sun with all the trees and beauty of nature around me.

As I mentioned before, everything gets better with practice, so start practicing your gratitude. The best way is to do it at the beginning or end of each day. It doesn't have to be in a written form but can be a reflection. If you're really serious about it, you can also start a gratitude journal and write down all your daily blessings and nice moments in your life, even small ones like the fragrance of your flowers. When you need a lift, you can go back to your journal and read it. It will instantly make you feel better. Oprah Winfrey has mentioned her gratitude journal in interviews. Research also shows that sharing your grateful attitude with a friend will make you both feel better, so why not do it?

One of the most influential contemporary teachers and writers on gratitude is a ninety-three-year old Benedictine monk, David Steindl-Rast (2016 and 2018), who said, "Want to be happy? Be grateful." Every day brings a lot of moments that may not be exactly positive experiences, but it's important not to dwell on those moments and to have a grateful attitude. This means being grateful for all the experiences that come into your life, since they're here to teach you something about yourself or the universe that we're an integral part of.

I agree with Geneen Roth, author of the 2018 book *This Messy Magnificent Life: A Field Guide*, that practicing gratitude several times a day is a good way to go through life. It can especially help if you are having a difficult time, a day when "bad things" just keep coming at you. If you take a little time to think about the good things, or all the blessings that you have in life, it makes your attitude a lot better almost instantly. You can think about good health if you have it, your family, or just the sunshine or the color of the sky. I love to think about the colors of my roses in the morning sun and other flowers in my garden. I believe that the colors of nature are the most incredible and difficult to replicate, even by the most advanced technology.

I also like the idea of Cheryl Richardson, a life coach and best-selling author of the 2017 *Waking Up in Winter: In Search of What Really Matters at Midlife*, that self-care is a necessity, and an important part of self-care is focusing on the positive. I like her "pleasure list" of ten things that brought her pleasure each day. It can be something very small, and doesn't need to cost money, like playing with her cat or holding her husband's hand. The list has made her more aware of pleasurable everyday moments. It will be difficult at first, so start with one to three small things. With practice, you'll find plenty of them every day, and it'll make you feel better.

If you don't have time or energy to write lists at the end of the day, try to take a moment before you go to sleep to think about positive things in your life or things that you're grateful for. It can be a "cream of the cream" for your brain. As the late Dr. Wayne W. Dyer was teaching, your brain will be "marinating" in sleep for many hours. Therefore, it is important that it is marinating in positive, not negative, thoughts.

If you have a "down moment," please always remember what the Reverend DeVon Franklin once said: "Every day above the ground is a great day."

~26~
The Practice of Meditation

MEDITATION IS THE ACTIVITY OF SITTING QUIETLY AND directing your attention. It is the most effective practice for stress-reduction, relaxation, self-reflection, self-awareness, and generally maintaining well-being. According to the "guru" of meditation, Dr. Deepak Chopra (2014), meditation allows you to get in touch with your inner self, your consciousness, or your "cosmic self."

A great deal of research proves meditation's effectiveness. It suggests that meditation is at least as effective as medications for many mental health problems such as anxiety, depression, and ADHD. It can also boost your immune system, improve memory, and shrink brain centers associated with anxiety and stress. Research by Dr. Rudolf Tanzi (Chopra&Tanzi 2015 & 2018) indicates that meditation can affect gene expression

Rose garden can be a nice place to meditate (author's meditation place).

(gene regulation). It can down-regulate genes that cause diseases and up-regulate genes that facilitate health.

There are many forms of meditation (e.g., Transcendental, Buddhist, Zen, Tibetan, guided, visual, etc.). Internet research will help you pick the ones that suit you best. I believe that any form of meditation will relax you and improve your mental health and well-being. The most important thing is just to start doing it. Try to continue regularly, but don't feel guilty if you skip a few days. Go back to it when you can.

Dr. Chopra is reported to meditate every day from 4 to 8 a.m. That's a lot of time. Most of us can't spend four hours meditating, but as I mentioned before, even a few minutes daily will help. I practice meditation myself and encourage all my patients to do it for stress reduction and well-being.

When I start talking to patients about meditation, their reactions are similar: that they don't have time for it or tried it and it didn't work, so they're reluctant to try it again. When we talk about it more, it turns out that they have faulty assumptions about meditation. They usually have an image of somebody like a Buddhist monk sitting and meditating for hours, and they don't see themselves doing this. My response is to just try sitting quietly and breathing for five minutes once or twice a day. When you're comfortable doing it for five minutes, gradually increase the time.

The other most common complaint is that meditation doesn't work since it's impossible for them to just sit and think about nothing. I agree with that. The moment you sit down and try to meditate, a lot of thoughts will start coming to mind about your day, family, work, what you need to do next, etc.—and this is *normal*. As French philosopher Rene Descartes (1596-1650) said, "I think; therefore I am."

Your mind will stop thinking only when you're dead or become an Enlightened Buddhist monk. I emphasize that the therapeutic benefit comes from the moment you realize that your mind drifted away and you bring it back to concentrating on your breathing. If you have difficulty concentrating on your breathing, light a candle and try to concentrate on the flame. Observe its movement, color, smell, etc. It will help take your mind from your thoughts so you can relax. You can also place your hand on your chest while breathing and concentrate on the movement of your chest. Observe your chest going up and down when the stream of life (air) is entering your body. Again, try to meditate daily; little by little, it will get much easier with practice. After a while, these moments of silence and being with yourself will become a much-needed daily routine. As singer/songwriter Wynonna Judd said: "Silence is refreshment for the soul."

Try "tea meditation" to help you relax before bedtime:
For all my patients who have difficulty falling asleep, I recommend tea meditation as an alternative to medications before sleep. Recent research shows that such medications should only be used occasionally, as they suppress your brain activity, which may cause problems with brain functioning if used for a long period of time. However, used occasionally, they're better than a sleepless night, especially if you have to go to work the next morning.

I encourage my patients to try tea meditation instead of sleeping pills for some time, and not to give up after one try. As with everything in life, it will get better with practice. I also do it myself if I've had a stressful day and want to go to sleep instead of thinking stressful thoughts, which interfere with falling asleep. The idea is simple and is taken from Zen Buddhist tea meditation. Zen monks can spend an hour or more drinking a cup of tea, but you don't have to do it for such a long time. Fifteen to twenty minutes may be enough. Some people, however, may need more time to relax and let it help them fall asleep.

Important: Do your evening hygiene before brewing your tea so that after the tea meditation, you can go straight to bed. Use herbs with relaxing and antianxiety properties, such as chamomile, valerian root, lemon balm, hops, or lavender. Find out which works best for you. You can make your own combination of herbs or buy already-made sleep herb combinations at a health food store.

My favorite is valerian root, which has been used as an antianxiety aid and sleep remedy for generations in Europe, usually as valerian root drops. Research shows that valerian root is as effective as benzodiazepines in treating anxiety and helping a person relax, but without the side effects. Valerian root has a distinctive but not offensive smell, and less of it in ready-to-use formulations.

Brewing herbal tea is as simple as making regular tea: Pour boiling water into a cup with tea, cover it, and wait a few minutes. Find a quiet place in your home, a comfortable armchair, and a warm blanket if you live in a cold climate. Wait until the tea is warm, not hot. Sit in the chair, take the lid off, and hold the warm cup of tea in both hands, close to your mouth and nose. Sip a little and then inhale the vapor and breathe. Continue sipping it and inhaling the vapor until the cup is empty or you feel you're ready to go to bed. If you find yourself thinking about problems of the day, what you need to do tomorrow, or something that's disturbing you, bring your attention back to sipping and inhaling again and again. Try to concentrate on the taste and smell. How does the taste of the tea make you feel? How wonderful is the smell of the tea, which was given to us by Mother Nature. Think any relaxing and peaceful thoughts that come to mind. As you do it several times, concentrate on just sipping and inhaling. My patients like it, so I encourage you to try it and *have a good night's sleep.*

A guided visualization exercise to help you stop worry and other intrusive, unwanted thoughts:
This is the exercise that I teach all my patients who worry too much. The idea comes from writer and spiritual teacher Gary Zukav, whose best-known book is probably *The Seat of the Soul*, published in 1989. All his books are interesting, and I encourage you to read them. Many years ago, on *The Oprah Winfrey Show*, he talked about human consciousness, intuition, and authentic power. He gave an example of visualizing the mother ship and small ships that follow her. I liked the visualization of small ships in the ocean. I felt it could be calming to people and started thinking of how I could incorporate it into my life and clinical practice.

After some thinking and practicing on myself, I came up with the following mental exercise. What I teach my over-worried patients is that when their worrying thought comes to mind, they need to take a moment and visualize a big ocean with a few little boats in it, each a different color. They need to pick one of them, for example a blue boat, put the worrisome thought in that boat, and then visualize the boat with the thought in it sailing away in the ocean. When the worry thought comes back, say to it, "You're in the blue boat sailing away in the ocean." Repeat this several times if you're still having the thought. It helps break the cycle of worry. My patients have found it helpful, so it may also help you.

A guided visualization and meditation exercise to help you lessen or stop pain:
This is an exercise that I do myself and also teach my patients. It may sound somewhat unreal, but if done in a meditation-like state, it really works. However, it may take many times before some of you benefit. I took the idea from an early book by actress and writer Shirley MacLaine. (I've read almost all her books, and really like them.) She's done similar forms of meditation for hurting knees, and the pain disappeared. Though it took her only one try to get better because she's meditated for many years, the beginner may need several, but it's worth it to try. It costs nothing and has no side effects, unlike most pain medications.

When you feel a pain, sit the same way you usually do when meditating. If you don't meditate but want to try this mental exercise, sit in a comfortable position on the floor or a chair with your back straight and hands in your lap or in the meditation position (thumb touching a finger), whatever is more comfortable. If you have difficulty sitting with your back straight, just sit comfortably. Close your eyes and concentrate on your breathing. Follow your breath. After a moment, you'll realize that your body is relaxing. Try to relax the part of your body that's hurting.

Then visualize a blue sky and turn your attention to something like an imaginary center of the universe or God or any other entity that you believe is the spiritual center of the universe. Visualize a ball of bright, warm blue light coming down from that center. Imagine that the ball of light is traveling from the sky through the clouds down to the Earth and lands on the top of your head. Then it enters your body and travels to the part that's hurting and sits there for a while. After a moment, you may feel that the part of your body that hurts is getting warmer and more relaxed, and you may feel less pain.

Please be advised that I'm not suggesting this is a 100 percent guaranteed treatment for pain. I'm only saying that if you try it several times, it may lessen your pain without medications or you may get a break from your pain for a while. A break from pain sounds wonderful for somebody like me who suffers from scoliosis and used to have chronic pain. I don't take pain meds. I stretch, exercise, and meditate. When my pain comes back, I do this mental exercise again, and it always helps. Some people, like MacLaine, were able to heal themselves from pain permanently. I believe it's possible, but for me, there's still a long way to go. However, as I said before, a break from pain even for a few days is a wonderful thing.

Practice relaxation—aromatherapy:

Aromatherapy has been around for ages to help with many things, mainly stress reduction and relaxation. Many plants have beautiful scents and may relax you. The essential oils of certain plants used in aromatherapy may relax your mind and body, but most of them are expensive. You really don't need expensive essential oils to relax but can use a leaf or flower from plants you grow yourself. I teach my patients to grow some of them in pots and enjoy them free.

For relaxation, lemon balm and lavender plants can be very helpful. They grow well and are carefree except for watering when the soil is dry, which isn't often. You can buy small plants in local nurseries and plant them in a pot or your garden. When you feel stressed, pick a couple of leaves or flowers of lemon balm or lavender. Sit in a quiet place and rub the leaves or flowers between your hands. Then inhale their beautiful smell slowly, several times. It will relax you. Try it.

I have a few other suggestions: A friend uses lavender essential oil in a spray to help her children fall asleep, and she swears it works. I use lavender in my office to help anxious patients feel more relaxed. I make bouquets from my garden lavender when it's in bloom and arrange them around my office. I also sometimes spray lavender oil around me at the end of a long and stressful workday. It instantly makes me feel better.

~27~
Getting in Touch with Your Spiritual Self

TO IMPROVE, PRESERVE, OR HEAL YOUR BRAIN FUNCTIONING, you need to concentrate on your body, mind, and spirit. We've discussed body and mind, and now it's time to talk about your spiritual self.

What is spirituality?
Spirituality is not a religion. You can be very religious and still not be spiritual. You can also be spiritual but not associated with any religion. Of course, some religious people are also very spiritual.

There are many definitions of spirituality. For the purposes of this book, you can consider yourself spiritual if you feel connected to the universal power, the source of everything—what some people call *God*.

Research shows that people who believe in God and do spiritual practice daily or a few times a week feel better and are healthier. Although spiritual practice doesn't necessarily mean attending church services, if that helps you feel better and more peaceful, definitely continue doing it.

The two important components of spiritual practice are prayers and meditation, and you can also do meditating prayers. In addition, I strongly believe that whatever you do as a service to others with their best interests at heart is a spiritual practice. If your work requires you to serve others, and you do it having their best interests at heart, your work is also your spiritual practice.

The best way to get in touch with your spiritual self, which is a *God* element in you, is through meditation. (See Chapter 26.) Staying in touch with your spiritual self will be your lifelong journey, as your spirituality and relationship with God evolve. You will have days when you feel more connected and others when you feel less so or maybe even disconnected. This happens. Even one of the most spiritual people on Earth, Mother Teresa, had periods of doubt and feelings of disconnect which she called "dark nights." It's most important to stay connected to the source, God, and not to get off the road toward your better self despite changing circumstances.

Some people set spiritual goals for themselves. You can try doing that if you think it will help you on the journey.

~28~
The Power of Kindness and Compassion

Kindness is loving people more than they deserve.
—Joseph Joubert

EVERYBODY SEEMS TO KNOW WHAT KINDNESS MEANS. Generally, it's a tendency to feel concern for others. However, in our busy and stressful lives, we don't always remember to practice it. Compassion literally means "to suffer together." It means feeling or showing sympathy and concern for others and also includes the desire to alleviate their distress. The Dalai Lama once said, "If you want others to be happy, practice compassion. If you want to be happy, practice compassion."

Research shows that practicing kindness and compassion daily helps you be healthier. Compassion and little acts of kindness can make a big difference. However, don't feel guilty if you had a bad day and weren't kind or compassionate enough. Try again the next day. Life can be difficult, and even Jesus said that in this earthly life, we will have trouble (John 16:33). Don't forget that others have bad days as well, and theirs may be even worse. We don't know until they tell us. If somebody is rude to you, it's about them, not about you. You can answer them with kindness and compassion.

Whether you believe in karma, which is a spiritual law of cause and effect in Eastern religions, or just observe the laws of the universe, you know that any act of kindness and compassion that you do for another person will come back to you. The same is true with bad acts and unkindness. It may not necessarily be immediate, or it may come in a different form, but it will show up in your life. If you helped another person get through a difficult day, somebody else may help when you have a flat tire. Or when you're sick, a neighbor may shovel snow from your driveway. This is the true power of kindness and compassion.

Don't forget to be kind and compassionate to yourself. Research suggests that self-compassion may protect against stress-induced inflammation and inflammation-related disease (Breines, J. G. et al. 2014). Treat your body well by eating healthfully, exercising, practicing mindfulness, and doing other things that make you feel good about yourself. If you're kind and compassionate to yourself, it will be easier to have the same attitude toward others.

Also, if you want to change bad habits or behaviors, instead of beating yourself up, start with self-compassion. According to a study from the University of California at Berkeley, people who practice self-compassion are more motivated to improve themselves (Breines, J. G. and Chen, S. 2012). You can also practice compassion by volunteering to work with people or animals in need, giving money to a charity, or simply being a shoulder to lean on for someone. It will instantly make you feel better.

Being compassionate to yourself also means not overextending or overcommitting yourself at the expense of your physical and/or emotional health. Be compassionate to yourself first. You don't need to drive your friend to the airport on a day when you have multiple commitments, and you don't have to agree to do another retreat for your church if you've already done a few and have other commitments. If you feel that you have too much on your plate, you probably do and need to slow down to keep your sanity. Being stressed out, frustrated, and tired most of the time isn't good for you and the people around you. It will cause unnecessary stress, tension, and conflicts in your social environment.

I have a few friends who are doing way too much, and their health is failing. This is especially true of women who work full-time and have families to care for, houses to clean, and dinners to cook, and also are doing a lot for their church. They feel that they cannot say no. When they complain about their busy lives, I remind them about being compassionate to themselves first and finding time to rest and rejuvenate. It will pay off for both them and their social environment.

~29~
The Power of Inspiration

TO INSPIRE OTHERS, YOU NEED TO KEEP YOURSELF INSPIRED. How can you do this? Look for inspiration in books, art, your favorite shows, and people who were able to overcome the impossible. For example, Helen Keller (mentioned earlier), who became the first deaf and blind person to get a college degree, or more recently, Mandy Harvey, a deaf woman who became a successful singer/songwriter.

One show that always inspires me is *Super Soul Sunday* on OWN, the Oprah Winfrey Network. Oprah talks to people who can be called spiritual leaders of our times. They come from different backgrounds and parts of the world, and always have important and inspirational things to say about their own lives and their spiritual experiences. Sometimes, their way of thinking is so dense and intense that I listen to parts of the show several times. I want to get the real meaning of what was said because it always opens doors in my mind and focuses my attention on something that I either didn't know or wasn't thinking about in the way it was presented. The program always makes me ponder what's said, and I use it in my life and my work with patients.

Nature is a great inspiration and has motivated artists, poets, writers, and ordinary people for ages. You don't have to look far for it. Nature is all around you. It may be a view of an old tree from your window or flowers in your backyard. I love to meditate in my rose garden and listen to the water of my little fountain and the birds that take baths in it. You only need to look around, and you'll find the beauty of nature there. So keep observing it, and thank God (or the universe) for the ability to see and experience it. You can also be inspired by your favorite animals when they tirelessly try to cheer you up at the end of a difficult day.

How to inspire others? You don't have to be a famous person, artist, writer, or hero to inspire others. I believe that we can be the greatest inspiration when we're our true or authentic self. This may sound like "big words," and you can find many definitions, but for me, it's really simple. We need to function in our everyday life in accordance with our true values and have a sense of peace about who we are. This doesn't mean we're so content with ourselves that we "sit pretty" and stop working on our internal development. Just the opposite. We continue our spiritual, personal, and/or professional journeys toward our goals, whatever they are, but we always check to see if they're in alignment with our core values. We also need to honor our true feelings and needs and not be afraid of being real and genuine. This requires honesty and openness and may put us in uncomfortable situations. However, if you truly know who you are, nobody can take that from you because it is the real, true, and genuine substance of who you are.

How can you find out about your true and authentic self? It can be one of your goals in therapy or can be done in meditation or observation while interacting with other people. How others react to us and our behavior can tell a lot about who we truly are. It's refreshing to be around someone who feels true to his or her sense of values. To inspire people, you need to have a passion in life that benefits others and the universe. We are part of the universe, and whatever we do has an impact on it, whether we realize it or not. Therefore, we need to be conscious of our actions.

You may ask, "Can I inspire others if I'm struggling to recover from my brain trauma?" Yes, you can. There are no guarantees in life, but if you commit yourself to getting better and remain in a positive mood despite obstacles, you have more of a chance to recover better and faster and inspire your family, friends, and health care providers. You can even write a book about your journey to recovery in order to inspire others.

Take the example of two women who recovered quite well from severe brain traumas. Amy Cuddy was injured in a car accident and later became a Harvard professor, researcher, and author of a 2015 book on body language titled *Presence: Bringing Your Boldest Self to Your Biggest Challenges*. Another example is Jill Bolte-Taylor, a brain researcher who suffered a massive stroke at thirty-seven and was able to return to her profession. As mentioned earlier, she wrote a beautiful and inspirational book in 2008 about her experiences titled *My Stroke of Insight: A Brain Scientist's Personal Journey*.

You don't have to look far to find someone to inspire you. Such people are usually in your social environment. It may be somebody from your family such as your mother or a cousin who went back to school and got a college degree despite being a single mom of four. It can be your friend who beat cancer and does well despite a sad prognosis or a neighbor who decided to follow her dreams, quit a boring job, and taught English in underdeveloped countries. These people are all around us. We just need to take a closer look.

* * *

Let me share two examples of friends who inspired me. One, a therapist, was in an almost-fatal hit-and-run accident on a freeway about a year and a half ago. The driver responsible was never found, but my friend had brain trauma and severe bodily injuries. She was in the ICU for days, underwent several surgeries to fix broken bones, and spent months in two rehab hospitals before she could come home and take care of herself.

Despite these difficult experiences, she never lost her upbeat spirit. She was committed to getting better as soon as possible, and worked hard on her recovery. What was fascinating and inspiring for me was her commitment to keeping herself in a positive emotional state despite the obstacles. I never heard her complaining or asking, "Why me?" She was always grateful that she had survived the accident and was on her way to recovery. She forgave the driver who caused her injuries and was never angry with that person.

Also powerful and inspirational was her ability to guard against negativity that could have affected her spiritual well-being. Once, when talking on the phone while she was still in the hospital, I mentioned a mutual friend's difficult situation. The injured woman immediately reminded me that she wasn't in an emotional space to talk about that now. Her response struck me and gave me a lesson. She was right. I shouldn't have brought negativity into her emotional space. She recovered quite well and returned to her work as a therapist.

My other example is a friend who always has inspired me. She is a strong believer in God, and what is most important, she lives her life in faith, which isn't that common. Her whole life is an inspiration to others. She prays a lot and does a lot of good work for her church and for others, and always tries to follow Jesus in everything she does.

A wife, mother of six (one adopted), and grandmother, she used to work as a teacher. Many years ago, her daughter, who was becoming a nun, was volunteering at an orphanage in a remote location in South America. A severe hurricane left most of the land there either underwater or under mud. Many people lost their lives. For more than a week, my friend had no idea whether her daughter was alive, since there was no communication.

When I heard about the hurricane, I called to ask if she knew what had happened to her daughter. What she said had a profound effect on me. I'd never heard anyone talk like this, with such a strong faith and internal calm in the face of the possible tragedy of losing a child. My friend said, with total peace in her voice, I don't know, but I know that *He* (God) knows what has happened to her, and that's enough for me."

I can only hope that with time and practice, I'll be able to have such a strong faith and the internal peace she has. It's my long-term goal.

~30~
Strive for Progress, Not Perfection

SOME PEOPLE AREN'T SATISFIED WITH COMPLETING THEIR tasks or with their life in general until, in their opinion, they've done it in a perfect way. I see this often in my clinical practice. Some patients strive for perfection while doing testing, making many corrections and frequently being unable to finish on time.

Perfection can be a stumbling block on the road to your brain's recovery. After any kind of brain trauma, some cognitive functions can be compromised. Most of my patients are naturally concerned about whether they'll be able to return to their previous level of functioning. Unfortunately, there is no easy answer. In my over thirty years of practice, I've seen patients with severe brain traumas who were able to regain most of their functions and live a normal life. But I also remember a few who had minor brain traumas that worsened other conditions, such as medical problems or chronic mental illness, and they had difficulty functioning in everyday life.

I recommend that my patients who have suffered any kind of brain trauma concentrate on making steady progress instead of trying to make every step perfect and constantly comparing themselves to the person they were before the trauma. Such comparison leads to anxiety and depression, since recovery can take a long time. Also, some cognitive and motor functions may never recover to the previous level, but the patient still may be able to function quite well in everyday and professional life and enjoy living.

Progress is what counts in life. Don't be discouraged if you've had a bad day or had to take a few steps backward to make one step forward. It's still progress. Do it at your own pace with your own goals in mind. Try to make your goals measurable and put a time frame on them. And what is most important, give yourself a reward for reaching them even if you had to work on them longer than you had expected.

~31~
Concluding Remarks

I WROTE THIS BOOK FOR YOU, MY READER, WHETHER YOU'VE ever had or haven't had brain problems. I want to inspire you to start and continue your journey toward a healthy, well-functioning brain, which will help you reach your full potential and self-fulfillment in life.

The book is based on over sixty years of my personal experience and over thirty years of my professional experience, which I wanted to share with you.

Since some people like to start reading a book from the end, I want to mention that in the first part of this book, I explained in detail what a neuropsychological evaluation is and how it can help you, your family, and your health care providers. The second part is devoted to brain health.

Based on my personal and professional experience and contemporary knowledge, I described what I believe can be helpful to keep your brain working well to the end of your life. Since I like to cook healthy meals, I also shared some of my favorite family recipes for healthy eating. I believe that good physical health and a well-functioning brain are essential for our ability to take care of ourselves as we age. Nobody wants to become a burden to their family or, God forbid, end up in a care facility (unless you have a lot of money to afford a good one).

Not everything depends on us, and there is no guarantee in life, but if we try to follow a healthy diet, practice mindfulness, and stimulate our brain by doing cognitive and physical exercises and participating in social activities, we're putting our brains on the "good preservation program."

Let me leave you with a thoughtful quote from prominent businessman and author Harvey Mackay,

Life is too short to wake up with regrets. So love the people who treat you right. Forget about those who don't. Believe everything happens for a reason. If you get a chance, take it. If it changes your life, let it. Nobody said life would be easy, they just promised it would most likely be worth it.

And good luck on your journey to brain health.

References

Bachmann, Katharina, Alexandra Philomena Lam, Peter Sörös, Manuela Kanat, Eliza Hoxhaj, Swantje Matthies, Bernd Feige et al. "Effects of Mindfulness and Psychoeducation on Working Memory in Adult ADHD: A Randomised, Controlled fMRI Study." *Behaviour Research and Therapy.* 106 (July 2018): 47–56.

Bavishi, Avni, Martin D. Slade, and Becca R. Levy. "A Chapter a Day: Association of Book Reading with Longevity." *Social Science and Medicine.* 164 (September 2016): 44–48.

Benedict, Christian, Samantha J. Brooks, Joel Kullberg, Richard Nordenskjöld, Jonathan Burgos. Madeleine Le Grevès, Lena Kilander et al. "Association Between Physical Activity and Brain Health in Older Adults." *Neurobiology of Aging.* 34, no. 1 (January 2013): 83–90.

Billioti de Gage, Sophie., Bernard Bégaud, Fabienne Bazin, Hélène Verdoux, Jean-François Dartigues, Karine Pérès, Tobias Kurth, and Antoine Pariente. "Benzodiazepine Use and Risk of Dementia: Prospective Population Based Study." *BMJ* 345 (September 27, 2012): e.6231.

Bonaccio, M., A. Di Castelnuovo, G. Pounis, S. Costanzo, M. Persichillo, C. Cerletti, M.B. Donati et al. "High Adherence to the Mediterranean Diet Is Associated with Cardiovascular Protection in Higher, but Not in Lower Socioeconomic Groups: Prospective Findings from the Moli-Sani Study." *International Journal of Epidemiology.* 46, no. 5 (October 1, 2017): 1478–1487.

Bowtell, Joanna L., Zainie Aboo-Bakkar, Myra E. Conway, Anna-Lynne R. Adlam, and Jonathan Fulford. "Enhanced Task-Related Brain Activation and Resting Perfusion in Healthy Older Adults After Chronic Blueberry Supplementation." *Applied Physiology, Nutrition, and Metabolism.* 42, no. 7 (July 2017): 773–779.

Breines, Juliana G., and Serena Chen. "Self-Compassion Increases Self-Improvement Motivation." *Personality and Social Psychology Bulletin.* 38, no. 9 (September 2012): 1133–43.

Breines, Juliana G., Myriam V. Thoma, Danielle. Gianferante, Luke Hanlin, Xuejie Chen, and Nicolas Rohleder. "Self-Compassion as a Predictor of Interleukin-6 Response to Acute Psychosocial Stress." *Brain, Behavior, and Immunity.* 37 (March 2014): 109–14.

Buettner, Dan. *The Blue Zones: Lessons for Living Longer from the People Who've Lived the Longest.* National Geographic Society, 2008.

Caballero-Salazar, S., Leticia Riverón-Negrete, María Guadalupe Ordaz-Téllez, Fikrat Abdullaev, Jesús Javier Espinosa-Aguirre. "Evaluation of the Antimutagenic Activity of Different Vegetable Extracts Using an In Vitro Screening Test." *Proceedings of the Western Pharmacology Society.* 45 (February 2002): 101–103.

Chen, Pin-Liang, Wei-Ju Lee, Wei-Zen Sun, Yen-Jen Oyang, and Jong-Ling Fuh. "Risk of Dementia in Patients with Insomnia and Long-term Use of Hypnotics:

A Population-Based Retrospective Cohort Study." *PloS One.* 7, no. 11 (November 2012): e49113.

Chopra, Deepak. *Ask Deepak About Meditation and Higher Consciousness.* Brilliance Audio, 2014.

Chopra, Deepak, and Rudolph E. Tanzi. *Super Genes: Unlock the Astonishing Power of Your DNA for Optimum Health and Well-Being.* New York: Harmony Books, 2015.

Chopra, Deepak, and Rudolph E. Tanzi. *The Healing Self: A Revolutionary New Plan to Supercharge Your Immunity and Stay Well for Life.* New York: Harmony Books, 2018.

Corrada, Maria M., Joshua A. Sonnen, Ronald C. Kim, and Claudia H. Kawas. "Microinfarcts Are Common and Strongly Related to Dementia in the Oldest-Old: The 90+ Study." *Alzheimer's and Dementia* 12, no. 8 (August 2016): 900–908.

Cortese, Samuele, Maite Ferrin, Daniel Brandeis, Martin Holtmann, Pascal Aggensteiner, David Daley, and Paramala Santosh. "Neurofeedback for Attention-Deficit/Hyperactivity Disorder: Meta-Analysis of Clinical and Neuropsychological Outcomes From Randomized Controlled Trials." (2016). *Journal of the American Academy of Child and Adolescent Psychiatry.* 55, no. 6 (June 2016): 444–455.

Cramer, Holger, Dennis Anheyer, Felix J. Saha, and Gustav Dobos. "Yoga for Posttraumatic Stress Disorder—a Systematic Review and Meta-Analysis." *BMC Psychiatry* 18, no. 1 (March 22, 2018): 72.

Cuddy, Amy. *Presence: Bringing Your Boldest Self to Your Biggest Challenges.* Little, Brown and Company, 2015.

Dyer, Wayne W. *Wishes Fulfilled: Mastering the Art of Manifesting.* Hay House, 2012.

Edwards, Jerri D., Huiping Xu, Daniel O. Clark, Lin T. Guey, Lesley A. Ross, and Frederick W. Unverzagt. "Speed Processing Training Results in Lower Risk of Dementia." *Alzheimer's and Dementia: Translational Research and Clinical Interventions.* 3, no. 4 (November 2017): 603-611.

Elliot, Andrew J., and Daniela Niesta. "Romantic Red: Red Enhances Men's Attraction to Women." *Journal of Personality and Social Psychology.* 95, no. 5 (November 2008): 1150–1164.

Elliot, Andrew J. "Color and Psychological Functioning: A Review of Theoretical and Empirical Work." *Frontiers in Psychology* 6 (April 2, 2015): 368.

Erickson, Kirk I., Michelle W. Voss, Ruchika Shaurya Prakash, Chandramallika Basak, Amanda Szabo, Laura Chaddock, and Jennifer S. Kim et al. "Exercise Training Increases Size of Hippocampus and Improves Memory." *The Proceedings of the National Academy of Sciences* 108, no. 7 (February 15, 2011): 3017–3022.

Erickson, Karl I., Cyrus Raji, O.L. Lopez, James Becker, Caterina Rosano, A.B. Newman, H.M. Gach, Paul Thompson, A.J. Ho, and L.H. Kuller. "Physical Activity Predicts Gray Matter Volume in Late Adulthood: The Cardiovascular Health Study." *Neurology* 75, no. 16 (October 19, 2010): 1415–1422.

Erickson, Kirk I., and Arthur F. Kramer. "Aerobic Exercise Effects on Cognitive and Neural Plasticity in Older Adults." *British Journal of Sports Medicine* 43, 1 (January 2009): 22–24.

Franklin, DeVon. *Produced by Faith: Enjoy Real Success Without Losing Your True Self.* Howard Books, a division of Simon and Schuster, 2011.

Fung, Jason. *Obesity Code: Unlocking the Secrets of Weight Loss*. Greystone Books, 2016.

Fung, Jason. *The Complete Guide to Fasting: Heal Your Body Through Intermittent, Alternate-Day, and Extended Fasting*. Victory Belt Publishing Inc., 2016.

Gilbert, Elizabeth. *Eat Pray Love*. New York: Riverhead Books, an imprint of Penguin Random House LLC, 2006.

Grosso, Giuseppe, Stefano Marventano, Justin Yang, Agnieszka Micek, Andrzej Pajak, Luca Scalfi, Fabio Galvano, and Stefanos N. Kales. "A Comprehensive Meta-Analysis on Evidence of Mediterranean Diet and Cardiovascular Disease: Are Individual Components Equal?" *Critical Reviews in Food Science and Nutrition* 57, no. 15 (October 13, 2017): 3218–3232.

Gruson, Lindsey. "Color Has a Powerful Effect on Behavior, Researchers Assert." *New York Times* (October 19, 1982): 0001.

Harris, Dan. *Meditation for Fidgety Sceptics*. New York: Spiegel and Grau, an imprint of Random House, 2017.

Herbert, Anne, and Anna Esparham. "Mind-Body Therapy for Children with Attention-Deficit/Hyperactivity Disorder." *Children* (Basel) 4, no. 5 (May 2017): 31.

Hess, Nicole Catherine L., Gudrun Dieberg, James R McFarlane, and Neil A Smart. "The Effect of Exercise Intervention on Cognitive Performance in Persons at Risk of, or with, Dementia: A Systematic Review and Meta-Analysis." *Healthy Aging Research* (July 2014).

Homskaya, Evgenia D. *Alexander Romanovich Luria: A Scientific Biography*. New York: Kluwer Academic/Plenum Publishers, 2001.

Israili, Zafar H., and Sally J. Israili. "Tango Dance: Therapeutic Benefits: A Narrative Review." *International Journal of Advances in Social Science and Humanities*. 5, no. 9 (September 2017).

Jindani, Farah, Nigel E. Turner, and Sat Bir Singh Khalsa. "A Yoga Intervention for Posttraumatic Stress: A Preliminary Randomized Control Trial." *Evidence-Based Complementary and Alternative Medicine* 2 (September 2015).

Kabat-Zinn, Jon. *Guided Mindfulness Meditation*. Sounds True, 2005.

Kabat-Zinn, Jon *Wherever You Go, There You Are: Mindfulness Meditation In Everyday Life*. New York: Hyperion, 1994.

Kabat-Zinn, Jon. *Mindfulness For Beginners: Reclaiming the Present Moment—and Your Life*. Boulder Colorado: Sounds True, 2006

Kawas, Claudia H., Ronald C. Kim, Joshua A. Sonnen, Szofia S. Bullain, Thomas Trieu, and María M. Corrada. "Multiple Pathologies Are Common and Related to Dementia in the Oldest-Old: The 90+ Study." *Neurology* 85, no. 6 (August 2015): 535–542.

Keogh, J. Justin W.L. Andrew Kilding, Philippa Pidgeon, Linda Ashley, and Dawn Gillis. "Physical Benefits of Dancing for Healthy Older Adults: A Review." *Journal of Aging and Physical Activity*. 17, no. 4 (October 2009): 479–500.

Kirkorian, Robert, Marcelle D. Shidler, Tiffany A. Nash, Wilhelmina Kalt, Melinda R. Vinqvist-Tymchuk, Barbara Shukitt-Hale, and James A. Joseph. "Blueberry Supplementation Improves Memory in Older Adults." *Journal of Agricultural and Food Chemistry* 58, no. 7 (April 14, 2010): 3996–4000.

Krishnakumar, Divya, Michael R Hamblin, and Shanmugamurthy Lakshmanan. "Meditation and Yoga Can Modulate Brain Mechanisms that Affect Behavior and Anxiety—A Modern Scientific Perspective." *Ancient Science of Life.* 2, no. 1 (April 2015):13–19.

Lezak, Muriel Deutsch. *Neuropsychological Assessment* (3rd ed.). New York: Oxford University Press, 1995.

Longo, Valter D., and Mark P. Mattson. "Fasting: Molecular Mechanisms and Clinical Applications." *Cell Metabolism* 19, no. 2 (February 4, 2014): 181–192.

Luria, Aleksandr Romanovich. *Higher Cortical Functions in Man.* Moscow University Press, 1962.

Luria, A.R. *The Working Brain: An Introduction to Neuropsychology.* New York: Basic Books, 1973.

Macpherson, Helen, Wei-P. Teo, Luke A. Schneider, and Ashleigh E. Smith. "A Life-Long Approach to Physical Activity for Brain Health." *Frontiers in Aging Neuroscience* 9, (May 23, 2017): 147.

Mahendra, Poonam, and Shradha Bisht. "Anti-Anxiety Activity of Coriandrum Sativum Assessed Using Different Experimental Anxiety Models." *Indian Journal of Pharmacology* 43, no. 5 (September 2011) 574–577.

Mitchell, John T., Lidia Zylowska, and Scott H. Kollins, "Mindfulness Meditation Training for Attention-Deficit/Hyperactivity Disorder in Adulthood: Current Empirical Support, Treatment Overview, and Future Directions." *Cognitive and Behavioral Practice* 22, no. 2 (May 2015): 172–191.

Mitchell, John T., Elizabeth M. McIntyre, Joseph S. English, Michelle F. Dennis, Jean C. Beckham, and Scott H. Kollins. "A Pilot Trial of Mindfulness Meditation Training for ADHD: Impact on Core Symptoms, Executive Functioning, and Emotion Dysregulation." *Journal of Attention Disorders* 21, no. 13 (November 2017): 1105–1120.

Nagendra, Ravindra P., Nirmala Maruthai, and Bindu M. Kutty. "Meditation and Its Regulatory Role on Sleep." *Frontiers in Neurology* 3 (April 18, 2012): 54.

Northrup, Christiane. *Women's Bodies, Women's Wisdom: Creating Physical and Emotional Health and Healing.* New York: Bantam Books, 2002.

Panza, G.A., Beth A Taylor, Hayley V. Macdonald, Blair T. Johnson, Amanda L. Zaleski, Jill Livingston, Paul Daniel Thompson, and Linda S. Peccatello. "Can Exercise Improve Cognitive Symptoms of Alzheimer's Disease?" *Journal of the American Geriatrics Society* 66, no. 3 (March 2018):487–495.

Papandreou, Magdalini A., Andriana Dimakopoulou, Zacharoula I. Linardaki, Paul Cordopatis, Dorothy Klimis-Zacas, Marigoula Margarity, and Fotini Lamari. "Effect of a Polyphenol-Rich Wild Blueberry Extract on Cognitive Performance of Mice, Brain Antioxidant Markers and Acetylcholinesterase Activity." *Behavioural Brain Research* 198, no. 2 (March 17, 2009): 352–358.

Petersson, Sara Danuta, and Elena Philippou. "Mediterranean Diet, Cognitive Function, and Dementia: A Systematic Review of the Evidence." *Advances in Nutrition.* 7, no. 5 (September 2016): 889–904.

Pollan, Michael. *The Omnivore's Dilemma: A Natural History of Four Meals.* New York: Penguin Press, 2006.

Pounis, George, Simona Costanzo, Marialaura Bonaccio, Augusto Di Castelnuovo, Amaliade Curtis, Emilia Ruggiero, Mariarosaria Persichillo et al. "Reduced Mortality Risk by a Polyphenol-Rich Diet: An Analysis from The Moli-Sani Study." *Nutrition.* 48 (April 2018): 87–95.

Richardson, Cheryl. *Waking Up in Winter: In Search of What Really Matters at Midlife.* HarperOne, 2017.

Rosato, Valentina, Norman J. Temple, Carlo La Vecchia, Giorgio Castellan, Alessandra Tavani, and Valentina Guercio. "Mediterranean Diet and Cardiovascular Disease: a Systematic Review and Meta-Analysis of Observational Studies." *European Journal of Nutrition.* (November 25, 2017).

Roth, Geneen. *This Messy Magnificent Life: A Field Guide.* New York: Scribner (Simon and Schuster), 2018.

Rucklidge, Julia J., Chris M. Frampton, Brigette Gorman, and Anna Boggis. "Vitamin-Mineral Treatment of Attention-Deficit Hyperactivity Disorder in Adults: Double-Blind Randomised Placebo-Controlled Trial." *British Journal of Psychiatry.* 204, no. 4 (April 2014): 306–315.

Rucklidge, Julia J., Chris M. Frampton, Brigette Gorman, and Anna Boggis. "Vitamin-Mineral Treatment of ADHD in Adults." *Journal of Attention Disorders.* 21, no. 6 (April 2017) 522–532.

Shih, Hsin I., Che Chen Lin, Yi-Fang Tu, Chia-Ming Chang, Hsiang-Chin Hsu, Chih-Hsien Chi, and Chia Hung Kao. "An Increased Risk of Reversible Dementia May Occur After Zolpidem Derivate Use in the Elderly Population: A Population-based Case-Control Study." *Medicine (Baltimore)* 94, no. 17 (May 2015): e809.

Stanmore, Emma, Brendon Stubbs, Davy Vancampfort, Eling D. de Bruin, and Joseph Firth. "The Effect of Active Video Games on Cognitive Functioning in Clinical and Non-Clinical Populations: A Meta-Analysis of Randomized Controlled Trials." *Neuroscience and Behavioral Reviews.* 78 (July 2017): 34–43.

Staufenbiel, Sabine M., Anne-Marie Brouwer, A.W. Keizer, and Nelleke C. van Wouwe. "Effect of Beta and Gamma Neurofeedback on Memory and Intelligence in the Elderly." *Biological Psychology.* 95 (January 2014): 74–85.

Steindl-Rast, David. *Stop-Look-Go: A Grateful Practice Workbook and Gratitude Journal.* Wink Books Inc., 2016.

Steindl-Rast, David. *May Cause Happiness: A Gratitude Journal.* Boulder, CO: Sounds True, 2018.

Thich Nhat Hanh. *The Miracle of Mindfulness: An Introduction to the Practice of Meditations.* Boston: Beacon Press, 1975.

Uddin, Kamal, Abdul Shukor Juraimi, Sabir Hossain, Most. Altaf Un Nahar, Eaqub Ali, and Mosaddiqur Rahman. "Purslane Weed (Portulaca oleracea): A Prospective Plant Source of Nutrition, Omega-3 Fatty Acid, and Antioxidant Attributes." *Scientific World Journal* (2014).

Verghese, Joe, Richard B. Lipton, Mindy J. Katz, Charles B. Hall, Carol A. Derby, Gail Kuslansky, Anne F. Ambrose, Martin Sliwinski, and Herman Buschke. "Leisure Activities and the Risk of Dementia in the Elderly." *New England Journal of Medicine.* 348 (June 19, 2003): 2508–2516.

Verrusio, Walter, Evaristo Ettorre, Edoardo Vicenzini, Nicola Vanacore, Mauro

Cacciafesta, and Oriano Mecarelli. "The Mozart Effect: A Quantitative EEG Study." *Consciousness and Cognition.* 35 (September 2015): 150–155.

Weber, Miriam T., Leah H. Rubin, and Pauline M. Maki. "Cognition in Perimenopause: The Effect of Transition Stage." *Menopause* 20, no. 5 (May 2013): 511–7.

Woodyard, Catherine. "Exploring the Therapeutic Effects of Yoga and Its Ability to Increase Quality of Life." *International Journal of Yoga* 4, no. 2 (July–December 2011): 49–54.

Zamora-Ros, Raul, Viktoria Knaze, Leila Luján-Barroso, Isabelle Romieu, Augustin Scalbert, Nadia Slimani, Anette Hjartåker et al. "Differences in Dietary Intakes, Food Sources and Determinants of Total Flavonoids Between Mediterranean and Non-Mediterranean Countries Participating in the European Prospective Investigation into Cancer and Nutrition (EPIC) Study." *British Journal of Nutrition* 109, no. 8. (April 28, 2013): 1498–1507.

Zelinski, Elizabeth M., and Ricardo Reyes. "Cognitive Benefits of Computer Games for Adults." *Gerontechnology.* 8(4) (Autumn 2009): 220–235.

Zukav, Gary. *The Seat of the Soul.* New York: Fireside, 1989.

Zylowska, Lidia, Deborah L Ackerman, May Yang, Julie L. Futrell, Nancy L Horton, Sigi Hale, Caroly Pataki, and Susan L Smalley. "Mindfulness Meditation Training in Adults and Adolescents with ADHD: A Feasibility Study." *Journal of Attention Disorders* 11(6): (May 2008): 737–46.

Made in the USA
Middletown, DE
05 June 2021